Making
TIME
for Strategy

HOW TO BE LESS BUSY
AND MORE SUCCESSFUL

RICHARD MEDCALF

First published in Great Britain in 2023
by Xquadrant
In partnership with whitefox publishing

Copyright © Richard Medcalf, 2022

https://xquadrant.com
www.wearewhitefox.com

ISBN 978-1-915036-74-2

Richard Medcalf asserts the moral right to be identified as the author of this work.

All rights reserved. No part of this publication may be reproduced, stored in a retrieval system or transmitted in any form or by any means, electronic, mechanical, photocopying, recording or otherwise, without prior written permission of the author.

Designed and typeset by seagulls.net
Cover design by Mecob Design
Project management by whitefox

Contents

| CHAPTER 1 | Long days, slow progress | 1 |

Part 1
THE POWER OF STRATEGIC TIME — 7

CHAPTER 2	It's not busyness. It's the Infinity Trap	9
CHAPTER 3	Your #1 KPI	13
CHAPTER 4	Stop trying to free yourself up from things	17
CHAPTER 5	Next year's success formula	19
CHAPTER 6	The most important project is the one nobody is asking for	22
CHAPTER 7	I'm calling you up	26
CHAPTER 8	Choose your own adventure	28

Part 2
THE TACTICAL CHALLENGE   31

CHAPTER 9	It won't get quieter next quarter	33
CHAPTER 10	Define your starting point	38
CHAPTER 11	Set the boundaries	43
CHAPTER 12	Make the bold decisions	48
CHAPTER 13	Step 1: Cut	52
CHAPTER 14	Step 2: Reduce	55
CHAPTER 15	Step 3: Assign	57
CHAPTER 16	Step 4: Systematise	62
CHAPTER 17	Step 5: Hold	66
CHAPTER 18	You've built a perfect system for being busy	69
CHAPTER 19	Your $100 hammer	77
CHAPTER 20	Three minutes, not thirty minutes	85
CHAPTER 21	Now, do the work	88

Part 3
THE INFLUENCE CHALLENGE 91

CHAPTER 22 **The diet saboteurs** 93

CHAPTER 23 **Preparing for high-value conversations** 97

CHAPTER 24 **Scripts** 102

CHAPTER 25 **Daddy speaks English** 105

CHAPTER 26 **You're a leader, not Sherlock Holmes** 108

CHAPTER 27 **The 'Accept' button is the lazy option** 114

CHAPTER 28 **The magic of success checklists** 117

CHAPTER 29 **Tactics were never going to be enough** 121

Part 4
THE MINDSET CHALLENGE 123

CHAPTER 30 **It's all in your head, Mr Tweedy** 125

CHAPTER 31 **You're the High-Performing Janitor** 131

CHAPTER 32 **When trustworthy becomes untrustworthy** 134

CHAPTER 33 **You say responsive. I say distracted** 138

CHAPTER 34	What if the problem with your team... was you?	142
CHAPTER 35	You are productive... too productive	149
CHAPTER 36	You're addicted to firefighting	153
CHAPTER 37	Make contribution your North Star	156
CHAPTER 38	Be Superman. Or Batman	160
CHAPTER 39	**WWXD**	163
CHAPTER 40	Keep it front of mind	165
CHAPTER 41	On dragons and demons	169

Part 5
THE ENVIRONMENT CHALLENGE   175

CHAPTER 42	You say *agile*. I say *chaos*	177
CHAPTER 43	Work the system	179
CHAPTER 44	Six barriers to IMPACT	182
CHAPTER 45	Words are your weapon	186
CHAPTER 46	What are we not getting to?	189

CHAPTER 47	**Remove the chocolate from the mini-bar**	193
CHAPTER 48	**Clear, quick, convenient**	197
CHAPTER 49	**Making it matter**	201
CHAPTER 50	**Roadmap to revolution**	204

CONCLUSION 205

| CHAPTER 51 | **Two Paths** | 209 |

NEXT STEPS 213

ABOUT THE AUTHOR 215

CHAPTER 1

Long days, slow progress

'I'm overloaded, my team is overloaded, everyone is overloaded.'

You're not alone. All around you, leaders, teams and whole businesses are frantically scrambling to meet operational demands. Overloaded. Overwhelmed. Trying, and failing, to deal with an infinite number of calls upon their time.

You may say that 'infinite' is an exaggeration, but I don't think so. The way I see it, we live in a world of infinity. Technology has created a unique situation in human history, where every knowledge worker faces infinite demands and opportunities. There are infinite pulls on our time, infinite ways to build relationships, and infinite content to consume. If you're not convinced, go check your messages, your social media accounts, or your favourite streaming app. We are faced with infinite opportunities and possibilities.

And yet, we are mere mortals with very finite amounts of time, energy and attention. So how can you survive, and thrive, in this new world?

How can you extract yourself from the lower-value tasks that demand your attention, so that you can focus your thinking on the strategic projects that will deliver breakthrough results and a new level of performance?

For many top leaders, the problems are real and the stakes are high. 'I leave the office every day after twelve hours of work and I still don't feel I've made a dent in what I need to do,' said Mike, a client of mine. He is Chief Operating Officer at a large technology services company, running a global organisation. There are many moving parts. He has to deliver a big corporate transformation as well as achieve many short-term deadlines. He's up early, talking to one part of the world, and he works late, speaking with another. He's an incredibly capable leader, but the sheer complexity of his role has created real overload. For the first time, he's unsure whether he has what it takes.

This level of overload creates issues at home. His family would like more of his time. He does his best but he's always got a sense of being 'behind'.

What's more, being super-busy isn't serving him at work, either. When we're swimming in all the operational detail, we end up with tunnel vision and get stuck in busywork. We lose our capacity for real strategic thinking and we don't spot the opportunities and shortcuts that would get us to our destination faster and with far less effort. We're stuck on the hamster wheel.

As Mike said to me, 'Can I get above the detail enough to be successful?'

A roadmap to move from productivity to strategy

This book recognises that highly competent and successful leaders such as Mike – and you! – get overloaded and stuck in operations. In fact, the more competent you are, the more likely it is that you'll become the bottleneck in the system. This limits your overall impact and creates only incremental progress for both you and for your organisation.

So how do you break out from the incremental to the exponential? What will it take to get out of the weeds and make progress on the truly important issues?

Like most leaders, you've probably tried to implement advice about productivity and delegation. But productivity can't get you where you need to go. Productivity tells you to go faster, work harder, take on more. But none of this makes a dent in the infinity of demands. In fact, the faster you go, the more pulls on your time you have!

This book takes a different angle and addresses the real organisational barriers, mindset issues, technology drivers and behavioural factors that are stopping smart leaders – and their teams – from working on the most strategic topics. As an advisor to some of the world's most accomplished executives, I've repeatedly seen that becoming a more strategic leader isn't just a question of tips and tricks; it's a deeper journey of transformation and a personal leadership challenge.

As you make your way through the five parts of the book, you'll diagnose and overcome the real issues for you personally and for your organisation as a whole. This will help you to free up several hours of what I call 'Strategic Time' each week. **This is time spent on your most strategic and valuable activities, which will allow you to create real progress in your organisation,** whilst also improving the time you spend with friends and family.

Freeing up Strategic Time requires us to address four essential factors, which helpfully spell out the word TIME: Tactics, Influence, Mindset and Environment. We'll cover each of these critical components in the different parts of the book.

The scene is set in the first part of the book, *'The Power of Strategic Time'*. You will get clear about your personal opportunity for increased impact, and how what you think is desirable and productive behaviour may actually be harming your future success.

In *'The Tactical Challenge'*, you will learn to make bold moves to free yourself up in the short term whilst also building structures, systems and habits that will help you raise your game on an ongoing basis. Many leaders never put in place these basic disciplines, and suffer for it every day of their working lives.

In *'The Influence Challenge'*, you will examine how to bring your stakeholders on board, so that you can turn your plans into reality, and ensure that your new methods of working are supported and welcomed by your superiors, your reports, and your peers.

Then, in *'The Mindset Challenge'*, you will get to the root cause of your overload and your inability to make time for the most strategic topics. Whereas most leaders believe they have no choice given all the pressures and demands on their time, you will shift your thinking and address the fears, the people-pleasing, and the unconscious assumptions that are keeping you on the hamster wheel.

Finally, in *'The Environment Challenge'*, you will begin to shape the entire culture in your team and in the wider business, helping the organisation shift from the addiction of 'firefighting' to more impactful ways of working and collaborating. In other words, you'll create an environment where making time for strategy becomes more and more natural for everyone.

PROVEN KEYS TO UP-LEVEL YOUR IMPACT

These four challenges – tactics, influence, mindset, environment – are the topics that I regularly work with my clients on. In my previous roles – a partner in a top-tier strategic consulting firm, and as an executive at global tech giant Cisco – I saw time and time again that even the most accomplished executives and teams get snarled up in the operational quagmire, which results in incrementalism instead of bold and meaningful progress.

And now, as a trusted advisor to some of the world's most impressive founders, CEOs and their teams, I find that 'getting out of the weeds' is a top-of-mind topic for an astonishing number of these high achievers.

When I work with these extraordinary individuals and teams, our goal is generally to create an order-of-magnitude improvement in the impact they're making. This requires re-engineering a 'success formula' that's often already working extremely well. And one of the first obstacles that comes up, time and again, is operational overload and not having enough time to think and lead strategically.

This book, then, has emerged from deep client conversations. It's the result of seeing which shifts in perspective and which shifts in behaviour actually make a difference for busy business leaders. As you'd expect, these ideas have proven their value in the C-Suite, with clients including CEOs of multi-billion dollar corporations, executive teams in scale-up tech firms, award-winning entrepreneurs, and many more.

You don't need to be top dog to apply these ideas. The ideas in this book have also been tested by a broad cross-section of managers. They have participated in our public *Impact Accelerator* programme and learned to free up 5–10 hours per week for more strategic activity in just a couple of months.

TIME TO BEGIN

This book is for leaders who want to operate at a new level, extracting themselves and their teams from the mundane so they can work on the issues that matter.

It's for mere mortals who realise they cannot beat an infinite set of demands with productivity, but who are ready to arm themselves with strategy and courage.

It's for leaders who are ready to be world class.

This isn't a theoretical guide (because our goal is transformation, not just information) but it does spend time on key concepts. It's not a how-to manual (because you can Google a million productivity hacks), but it does give practical steps. And like any book, it won't do the work for you. I'll put the keys to more impactful, strategic activity in your hands, but you will need to unlock the door.

To help you get the most from the time you're investing in reading this book, we've prepared a number of bonus resources and interactive tools, including an action planning worksheet for each part of the book. You might like to head over to **https://xquadrant.com/bookbonuses** now so that you have them to hand and can work through them at the appropriate time.

So where do we start? Well, to thrive in our world of constant overload, we need to understand it – and understand ourselves. What are the unique challenges, traps and success requirements of this new context? It's there our journey begins.

Part 1

THE POWER OF STRATEGIC TIME

CHAPTER 2

It's not busyness. It's the Infinity Trap

I could tell by the speed she was talking that something was wrong.

'I need to speak to you about two things today. I've got a problem with a team member and a big meeting coming up with the Head of Region.'

This was Susanna, a Cambridge-educated superstar who'd been promoted at a young age to the UK leadership team of a major pharmaceuticals company just a few months before.

I tried to slow her down: 'OK, but how are you?'

'Fine really. Very busy, but all good,' came the predictable reply. I could feel our conversation was still rushing along at the surface level.

Over the next few minutes I slowed her down some more, and it started to come out. The overload. The days stuffed from beginning to end with meetings. The relentless deliverables. The Sundays that were the only time she had to actually do focused work. The adrenaline, and the exhaustion.

As we continued to talk, we explored the bigger picture. I probed: what were the big outcomes she was really hired to achieve? It turned out that there were two key objectives that only she could really make happen. She was making progress on one, but the other had practically fallen off her radar.

And as we talked further, she had another insight: it was well over a month since she'd spoken with her boss, the general manager. The result was a lot of operational activity but very little understanding of, and alignment with, her most important stakeholder.

Susanna was in 'superhero mode'. The new leader arrives, strikes a power pose, and declares to the organisation: 'Don't worry, people, I'm here now!' – only to immediately dive in to a million activities at once.

Of course, this relentlessly fast pace does get a certain level of result. It does make an impact. But we fall very quickly into what I call the Infinity Trap.

The Infinity Trap is when we're super-busy delivering on what we see as the operational necessities, but in reality we've succumbed to tunnel vision. We're laser-focused on this week's deliverables, but we've lost sight of the bigger picture.

Chao was in a similar position. He'd just been hired as the Chief Revenue Officer of an innovative and very rapidly growing Fintech firm. The CEO and the board were asking him to increase his short-term revenue goals; his team were asking him to crack open his address book and set up high-level meetings; and he was still in the process of finalising and socialising his strategic plan to triple revenues in a couple of years.

THE INFINITY TRAP

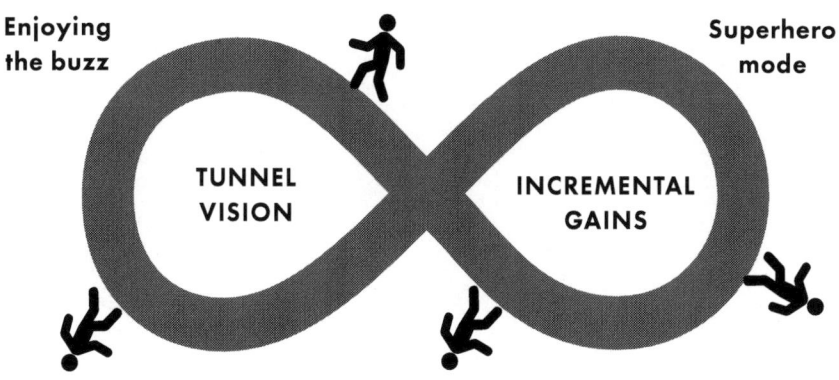

As a result, he was working seventeen-hour days. Enjoying the buzz, but feeling that something was missing and that he was losing control of his agenda.

During our conversation I focused Chao on the critical conversations that he needed to have to deliver a successful outcome in the next twelve months. It turned out that there was a make-or-break investment decision that would be taken by the CEO in an upcoming meeting. However, because he'd been so busy, this meeting wasn't getting the level of preparation it probably needed.

Again: superhero mode, overload, tunnel vision, and missing opportunities.

The Infinity Trap, once again.

As I've said, the demands on us are infinite. Every conversation begets another conversation. Every email stimulates more emails. We buy one book or watch one film, and ten more are proposed to us.

We think that sheer effort will see us through. And it's worked for us in the past. When you're in an operational role, head-down focus on deliverables often gets good results. But in leadership, where you're navigating complex, volatile and ambiguous situations, the Infinity Trap – tunnel vision – is deadly.

I invite you now to get honest with yourself. Where are you stuck in the Infinity Trap?

> *What's the one conversation that will change everything?*

There's a deeper question here. What's the payoff for you? What draws you in to the Infinity Trap? Personally, when I fall into busywork it's because there's a part of me that quite likes the adrenaline rush. For you, it might be the sense of being productive, being needed, or being in control. Realise that this is less about 'needing to be heads down right now due to short-term business pressures' and more about your own inner drive and habitual ways of operating. And when we change those, new possibilities for impact will open up.

I invite you to consider how the Infinity Trap is affecting you. Mentally zoom out. See yourself beavering away, trapped in busyness and suffering from tunnel vision. And then ask yourself, what are you not getting to? What's the one thing that will make everything else easier? What's the one conversation that will change everything?

Where are you stuck in the Infinity Trap?

CHAPTER 3

Your #1 KPI

As leaders, we live and breathe metrics and key performance indicators. However, in this world where there are infinite demands on your time there is one metric that is the determinant of your long-term impact and success. And the chances are that you're not giving it enough focus.

Let me illustrate with a story. It explains how I became the youngest-ever partner in the top-tier strategy consultancy where I started my career.

I joined as an analyst, and a big part of the job was building financial models and business plans in Microsoft Excel. These were often incredibly complex and detailed, and a core part of what we delivered to our clients.

Fast forward a couple of years; I was known for delivering top-quality and beautifully laid-out Excel models incredibly quickly, and had also taken on client management and business development responsibilities that my peers didn't have time to do.

What was the secret? Well, after a few months I realised I was repeating similar activities on every project. The financial models were all different, but I started to see commonality and repeated steps. So I started to build *infrastructure*. An Excel template with reusable 'modules' that I could copy and paste to quickly build all sorts of business plans.

A financial calculations sheet. Charts to present the key results in flexible ways. A toolbar that would allow me to apply complex formatting with just a keystroke or two.

This involved me working late for a couple of weeks, and most of my colleagues didn't understand why I was wasting time 'playing around' instead of doing client work.

But this investment quickly paid off. My business cases now looked better than anyone else's in the company, and I was building them incredibly efficiently. What took them a week took me a morning.

I was able to use the extra time to work on higher-value activities such as interpreting and presenting the results of the model, making recommendations, and engaging in sales and business development activities. And so my skill set up-levelled quickly, and the promotions followed.

WORKING HARDER IS NOT THE ANSWER

Most people attempt to tackle the challenges of an infinite workload by working harder, becoming more efficient, taking on more projects, solving more problems and addressing more customer demands. The problem is you rapidly hit what author and business coach Dan Sullivan describes as the 'Ceiling of Complexity', where there are no more hours in the day and you're wearing yourself ragged.

You're USING your time, and it's a hamster wheel.

Instead, *shift up a gear*. Instead of solving this month's/quarter's issues, work on different problems and projects, the things that will make next month/quarter/year/decade far more manageable and impactful.

You're INVESTING your time, and it's a flywheel.

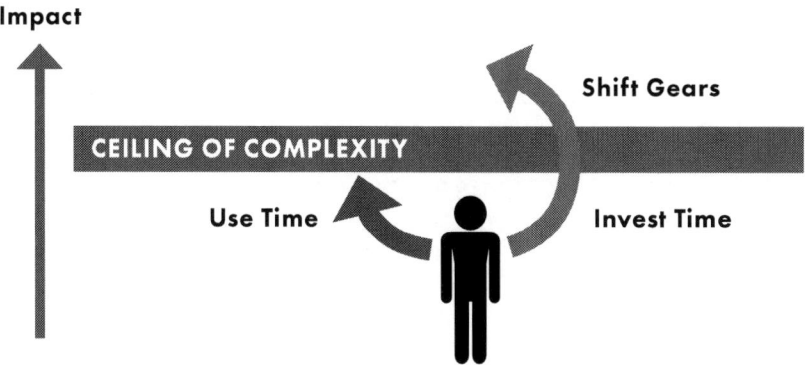

The problem is, most people are so busy on the hamster wheel they don't build the flywheel. They're using their time – engaging in the same kinds of tasks every time there's a new customer, a new project, a new quarter, a new financial year. It's never ending. They're not investing their time, building new capabilities and new relationships that will set themselves up for greater success in future.

> *Most people are so busy on the hamster wheel they don't build the flywheel.*

In that consulting company, the other analysts were busy on the hamster wheel, using their time on each project to build their financial models. I chose the 'short-term pain' of investing my time to develop templates and tools, but this became a flywheel that helped me build real momentum. It generated an incredible return on the time I'd invested, and it catapulted me forward in my career.

By freeing myself up, I'd created what I call *Strategic Time*.

STRATEGIC TIME IS YOUR #1 PREDICTOR OF FUTURE SUCCESS

Strategic Time: The hours in your week you invest on the 'up-levelling' projects that'll put you and your team in a far better place to deliver on your operational goals in the future.

Strategic Time is the #1 metric that determines your future success. You create a little bit (enough, in my case, to build my templates and tools) and use this to build new capabilities. This frees up even more time, which you can invest to up-level even more. In my case, this up-levelling took the form of client management and project management activities that were typically reserved for more experienced consultants.

Strategic Time, like any investment, creates a compound effect. In the world of finance, we see this clearly. You invest $1 today that brings a return tomorrow, and you reinvest that so you earn even more the day after. It's exponential.

If you're *using* your time, you're spending your days on tasks that need to be done, but those same tasks are basically going to reoccur. You're keeping the lights on, but you're not moving forward in a significant way.

However, if you've created Strategic Time, you're *investing* your time; you are working to create a permanent improvement in future. This is why it's your #1 predicator of future success.

Are you on the hamster wheel, or the flywheel? How many hours of Strategic Time do you have each week right now? How many do you want to have?

CHAPTER 4

Stop trying to free yourself up from things

'I became a delegation expert overnight...'

I've argued that the #1 metric that governs our future success is *Strategic Time:* time for important activities that eliminate risk, overcome bottlenecks, or build new capabilities.

But how do we actually create that time?

Most people start by trying to free themselves up from all the lower-level tasks around them. But it's the wrong approach.

It's almost impossible to free yourself up from low-value tasks. As the saying goes, 'Nature abhors a vacuum' – and we live in a world of infinity. So if we plough through our to-dos and manage to free up a few minutes, we just find more and more things to do. If you free up ten minutes, they'll just get swallowed up by the next task on the list.

So, stop trying to free yourself up from things. Instead, take a lesson from Billy.

INSTANT DELEGATION MASTERY

Billy D'Arcy is a telecoms-sector CEO, a previous client, and a former guest on my podcast, *The Impact Multiplier CEO*. In that interview, he explained how he achieved what I describe as 'instant delegation mastery'.

Billy's wife was taken into hospital, seriously ill, a few years ago. As he said, 'What that meant was that I had to rely much more on my own team, let go and actually get them used to doing meetings and events, and other really important stuff that I otherwise would have done myself.'

Because his real priority was suddenly very clear, the typical excuses and procrastination and half-hearted delegation tactics we all play with fell away. He freed up his time overnight to be with his wife, despite his natural tendency to be a very hands-on leader. And this lesson stuck with him.

So, be like Billy. *Don't try to 'free yourself up from' things. Instead, 'free yourself up to/for' things.*

Freeing yourself up *to/for* creates a purpose. You're not trying to create 'empty space' in your diary; you've got specific high-value activities and outcomes in mind that you're creating Strategic Time for.

The lesson here is simple. Don't start by worrying about how to extract yourself from the Infinity Trap and the incremental goals you're pursuing. Instead, begin by thinking about what you want to free yourself up for – those areas that will really catapult you forward and make a difference.

What are you trying to free yourself up for? What's the ultimate goal?

CHAPTER 5

Next year's success formula

'If you're doing the same things this year as you were last year, you're falling behind and probably failing.'
– Zoisa North-Bond, CEO, Octopus Energy Business & Generation (on the *Impact Multiplier CEO* Podcast)

It's so easy to run on tramlines.

Inertia takes over, and we find ourselves repeating the same behaviours that made us successful in the past. But, as the saying goes, *what got you here won't get you there.*

Forget about what made you successful last year. What are the behaviours that will make you successful next year?

If you look at your calendar and review how you spend your time, you'll typically find a mixture of $10/hour activities (such as tidying your inbox or popping out for an errand), $100/hour activities (which might include formatting documents or crunching some numbers), all the way up to activities with an hourly value of $10,000, $100,000, $1 million, or beyond.

What are the highest-value activities (HVAs) for you?

This isn't purely about monetary value. High-value activities are highly valuable and impactful to your stakeholders, and highly valuable, meaningful and fascinating to you.

They're going to stretch you, scare you, and stimulate you.

They are your path to impact.

> *High-value activities are highly valuable and impactful to your stakeholders, and highly valuable, meaningful and fascinating to you.*

One client, Lars, who founded and runs a hugely successful telecoms company, realised that his HVAs were (1) investor relations (2) developing and communicating vision and (3) catalysing the broader ecosystem in his industry to create societal impact. When we started working together, he realised he only spent about 10 per cent of his time on these activities!

Your HVAs can form a flywheel that makes exponential success almost inevitable. It's helpful to identify three HVAs, and then see if they reinforce and build on each other.

For example, my current HVAs are *creating* new content and fresh ideas, *connecting* with the world's top leaders, and *coaching* them to help them achieve a new level of impact. They reinforce each other: the more content I create, the more easily I can connect with high-level leaders; the more I connect, the more I end up coaching; and the more I coach, the better the content I create.

When you get specific about the high-value activities you want and need to be working on, you can start to free up time *for* them.

- » 'I'll free up time to define our next-gen partner strategy'
- » 'I'll free up time to develop some thought leadership'
- » 'I'll free up time to scope out my team development plan'
- » 'I'll free up time to work on my career move'
- » 'I'll free up time to win over stakeholders about the transformation project'
- » Etc.

Write down your 2–3 high-value activities (HVAs) for the coming year, and think about how they reinforce and build upon each other.

> *You can find worksheets to help you identify your high-value activities, along with the other resources for this book, at https://xquadrant.com/bookbonuses*

CHAPTER 6

The most important project is the one nobody is asking for

It felt like a wasted day.

I was about three months into my time at Cisco. Just starting to find my feet. I'd successfully completed my first customer engagement. And here I was, locked in my office, ignoring my to-do list and looking back at what felt like a day's pointless activity. I'd been trying to distil some of the learnings from the innovative work we'd just completed and make it relevant to a broader audience.

But I was tired, and a little demotivated. Why had I decided to spend the whole day doing some analysis that no one had asked for, and building a presentation no one was expecting? The deck wasn't even finished, so I didn't have anything to show for the effort. And there were plenty of colleagues and customers with more pressing demands on my time.

Fast forward a couple of months. The presentation had been shared at the highest levels in the company; I'd been asked to present it to some of the business's largest customers; I'd become a guest speaker at several major events. I'd started to put myself on the map.

I shouldn't have been surprised, really. Because the most important project is the one nobody is asking for.

YOU NEED TO HAPPEN TO *IT*

In the book *The 4 Disciplines of Execution*, authors Chris McChesney, Sean Covey and Jim Huling distinguish between the 'whirlwind of operations' – your day job – and your 'wildly important goals', which are new activities.

The whirlwind happens to you. It's loud. It's noisy. And, remember, the whirlwind is infinite. It will always be drawing you in, demanding more, requiring more.

But for your most important goals and projects, the opposite is true. *You will have to happen to them*!

Your most important project takes you out of business-as-usual and catapults you towards your breakthrough goals. It's not about meeting expectations, or even exceeding them: it's about making a leap forward.

Here are a few facts about your most important project (I call it an 'improvement project' to differentiate it from maintenance-style projects):

1. It's an investment. You invest Strategic Time now, and reap the rewards later.

2. Nobody is asking you for it.

3. If you don't make time for it, it will never happen.

4. It will make much of what you do easier or unnecessary in the future.

5. It is probably related to building new capabilities, new systems, new skills, or new relationships.

6. It's a project. So it needs a finish date and clear deliverable so you know when you're done.

7. You need momentum. So set a clear finish line (even to only complete a single phase of the project) within the next ninety days.

One of my clients, Gasheen, was completely overloaded and exhausted when we started working together. He had no time to work on his high-value activities. So we identified a single improvement project, which was to create the conditions necessary for a full delegation of two major recurring processes to his team. Within three months, he had freed up so much time that he was able to go to his manager and ask for additional responsibilities!

As Nicole Jensen said in our conversation on her *Leaders of Transformation* podcast, *'You can either be busy carrying water from the well to the village forever, or you can build a pipeline.'*

MAKE YOUR DAY A SUCCESS BY 10.30 A.M.

I'm writing this book, chapter by chapter, at the beginning of my working day. Nobody is asking for it; it's in the 'important but not urgent zone'. It's my #1 Improvement Project right now, so it comes first.

Why not make your day a success by 10.30 a.m.? Start your day by making progress on your #1 Improvement Project, the thing that nobody is asking for, the goal that will make everything else easier next week or next month. Then, secure in the knowledge that you've moved forward on your biggest goals, you can turn your attention to the whirlwind of operations.

The whole village is carrying the water from the well. No one's asking for it, but the path to impact is clear. You, my friend, go build the pipeline.

What is your top improvement project for the next ninety days?

CHAPTER 7

I'm calling you up

What I'm asking from you at this point is commitment.

Commitment is the seed from which everything grows, and it's the water that feeds the plant. Commitment is the start button and the fuel for the engine. Without commitment, we have nothing.

Commitment quickly becomes visible. If you look in your calendar, you'll see the things you are committed to in black and white.

And so the question for you is: are you committed to extracting yourself from the infinite operational pulls on your time? Are you committed to creating Strategic Time so you can make progress on more impactful projects? Are you committed to making changes in how you think, how you behave, and how you lead?

You've seen how the Infinity Trap can catch us. We become super-busy delivering on what we see as operational requirements, but in reality we've succumbed to tunnel vision and we've lost sight of the bigger picture. Are you committed to escaping the Infinity Trap?

You've learned about the importance of Strategic Time, and how it's the #1 metric governing your future success. You've seen how investing time

– rather than using time – is the only way to break through the Ceiling of Complexity. Are you committed to making some time investments, and multiplying your Strategic Time over the weeks to come?

You've discovered that trying to free yourself up *from* things is a dead-end. Are you committed to freeing yourself up *for* your high-value activities and your #1 Improvement Project? Whilst the whole village is carrying the water back and forth, are you committed to going and building the pipeline, the most important project that no one is asking for?

If you're in, then congratulations. A whole new future awaits.

CHAPTER 8

Choose your own adventure

Your journey to create Strategic Time will be different from everyone else's. However, you'll find the same building blocks need to be examined and reinforced. You'll need to focus on yourself (to build your own plans and habits, for example) and also focus on others (to secure their agreement and cooperation). Sometimes you'll need to take direct action, and other times you'll need to shift perspectives – your own mindset and the overall assumptions of the environment around you.

These two dimensions (action versus perspective, and self versus others) form the basis of the journey ahead, as the following diagram illustrates.

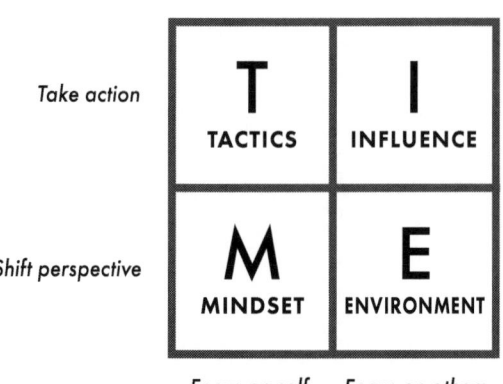

CHOOSE YOUR OWN ADVENTURE

You're pressed for time, so the good news is you don't need to read this book from cover to cover to start to benefit from it. You can dip straight in to whatever area is your #1 limiting factor right now, and get immediate benefits. Once you've worked on that area, come back here and decide what the next area of focus should be.

To be thorough about this, I do recommend you take the short online assessment at **https://xquadrant.com/bookbonuses/** which will give you an immediate recommendation about which area you should start with, and why.

Alternatively, you can just make a choice, and in the spirit of those classic *Fighting Fantasy* or *Choose Your Own Adventure* books of my youth, here are your options for where to go next:

» If you don't yet have a clear plan to make a significant and permanent dent in your operational workload, or if you simply want to work through things in order, then turn the page and dive into Part 2, *'The Tactical Challenge'*. You'll build a game plan to clear the decks of low-value work, and put in place the disciplines to keep you focused.

» However, making the decisions about what needs to happen isn't enough. If you know the tactical moves you need to make, but feel your stakeholders won't accept your plans, then skip forward to page 91 and Part 3, *'The Influence Challenge'*. You'll learn how to bring your stakeholders on board, so these changes are supported and welcomed by your superiors, your reports, and your peers.

» If you're not absolutely and viscerally *sure* that it's possible, necessary or desirable to extract yourself from operational concerns right now, then start with Part 4, *'The Mindset Challenge'* on page 123. We'll get to the root cause of your overload: the fears, the people-pleasing, and the unconscious assumptions that are keeping you on the hamster wheel and away from all the benefits of Strategic Time.

» Finally, if you find that your company culture is over-rotated to firefighting and incrementalism, and you want to think about how to help the broader organisation make more time for strategic activity, then head to page 175 and Part 5, *'The Environment Challenge'*.

Part 2

THE TACTICAL CHALLENGE

CHAPTER 9

It won't get quieter next quarter

> **'Do, or do not. There is no try.'** – Yoda

In this part, we're going to look at the Tactical Challenge, which is where you'll work on the skills and behaviours you'll need to actually free yourself up for more strategic activity.

There are three steps to this process.

First, you'll get clear on the journey ahead. What's your actual start point, and your desired end point? How focused is focused? How productive is productive? And when can you pause and declare success?

Second, you'll make some meaningful short-term improvements to get you to your desired end point. We'll introduce the CRASH methodology, and take you through that step-by-step.

Third, you'll set up some ongoing habits to maintain and build on this new level of strategic focus.

But first, we need to get one thing straight…

THERE IS NO 'PERFECT DAY'

Occasionally I decide to lose a bit of weight. Sometimes I'm successful, other times I'm not. I've come to realise there is just one decision that determines success or failure in the waistline department.

When I fail, it turns out that I'm waiting for The Perfect Day. And it turns out that almost no day is The Perfect Day for a diet! The reasons are endless:

- » We're at a nice restaurant.
- » Friends are coming over.
- » We're going to some friends.
- » It's the weekend!
- » It's my birthday.
- » It's your birthday.
- » We've got a lot of leftover cake.
- » I'm just a bit stressed today.

And the excuses go on. What I'm doing, of course, is fooling myself. When I think like this, I never get momentum and never get results because I'm delegating the hard work of *actually* dieting to my future self, who of course doesn't argue back. But when the future comes, and my future self is now my present self, I find myself confronted with the reality that I still don't want to buckle down and lose weight.

On the other hand, when I *commit*, then I do what it takes every single day to stay within my eating goals. And the results come, generally very quickly.

We do this all the time in business. The biggest lie we conspire to tell ourselves is: *it's crazy-busy right now but it should settle down next quarter.*

> **The biggest lie we conspire to tell ourselves is: 'it's crazy-busy right now but it should settle down next quarter.'**

But this isn't true. We live in a world of infinity, remember. The quieter times are *not* coming. It *won't* settle down next quarter. We have no idea what demand is going to come in, what issue is going to explode, how priorities will shift.

The Perfect Day idea struck a chord with Paul, a senior leader in one of my client organisations, a fast-growing IT infrastructure business. His top improvement project involved an organisational redesign, and he had made a few notes but hadn't progressed his thinking in months.

As we spoke, he realised that he was waiting for The Perfect Day, hoping it would get quieter next quarter. With that insight, he was able to develop a plan that forced him to make progress on this key project every single week. It made a huge difference.

ARE YOU READY TO START?

Have you ever seen the infographic *'Your Life in Weeks'*? It's astonishing and pretty scary to see every week of your life represented as a small but perfectly visible square on a single sheet of paper or your computer screen.

The point of the infographic? Every. Week. Counts.

Now let's think about *'Your Role in Quarters'*.

You know the speed at which the world is evolving. We're at an incredible moment in human history, with exponential technological progress creating so many challenges and so many opportunities – and things are moving fast. Miss the moment, and you miss the market.

The average employee tenure in a role is about three years. That's twelve quarters to make a real impact.

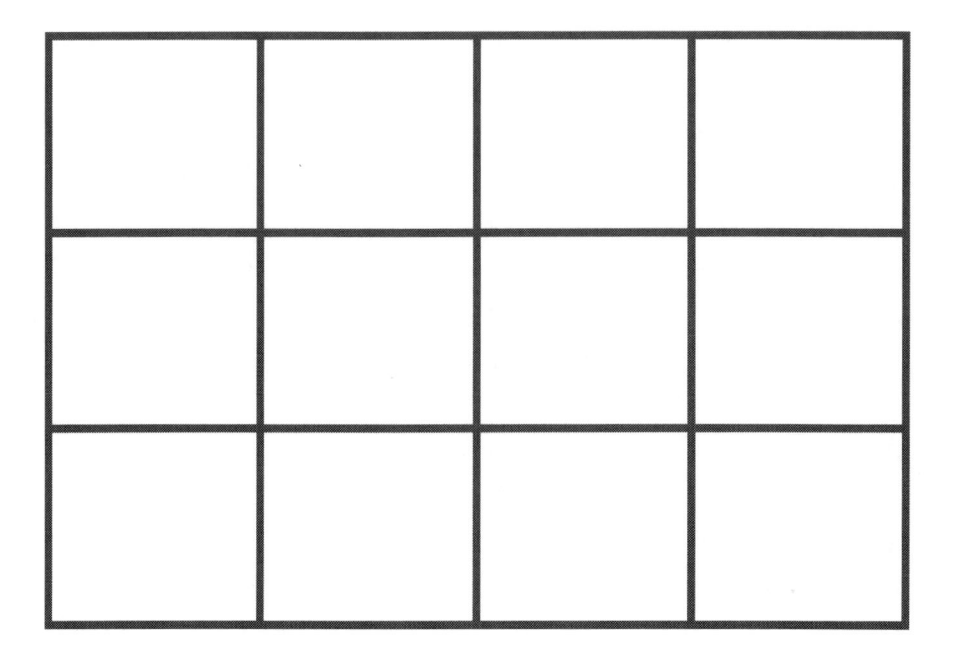

It's a small window of opportunity really when you look at it like that.

Every. Quarter. Counts.

So – where do you want to be in three years? How about two years? One year?

To create incredible results in twelve quarters you need to be investing THIS quarter so the return on that investment compounds exponentially over the remaining time.

Remember, twelve quarters is enough to do incredible things. It was enough for the England football squad to go from the humiliation of losing to Iceland in the 2014 World Cup to becoming a serious semi-final contender in 2018. And it was enough for Airbnb to scale from just over 10,000 users in 2010 to having served 9 million guests in 2013.

For most leaders, there's always an urgent issue to deal with. A fire to fight. It's never The Perfect Day (or The Perfect Quarter) and so they procrastinate and they never *start* on the things that will really create an order-of-magnitude improvement in their business.

Let's face reality. There is no Perfect Day. It won't get quieter next quarter. Your future self won't be any readier to take on the challenge than your current self.

So, are you committed enough to begin to pull yourself out of your tactical, operational concerns and focus on high-value-adding activities?

Are you ready to start, this quarter?

CHAPTER 10

Define your starting point

The first step in the Tactical Challenge is to understand your starting point. If you don't understand the current state of affairs, making meaningful process is very difficult.

Your goals reveal what your intentions are, but your calendar shows what you are committed to. So, get out your calendar and let's make a 'Commitment Inventory'.

This is a simple but revealing process. Simply list out, in some detail, your recurring activities according to their frequency: daily, weekly, monthly, quarterly, annually. Think about at least these categories: communications and messaging activity, tasks, meetings, people and projects.

For example:

Daily

- » Process email
- » Social media
- » Catch up on industry news

Weekly

- » Staff meeting
- » 1:1s with direct reports
- » Customer meetings
- » Coaching session
- » Business lunch

Monthly

- » All-hands meeting
- » Board call
- » Mastermind group

Quarterly

- » Sprint planning session
- » QBR

Annually

- » Team offsite
- » 1:1 appraisals/development conversations
- » Annual vacations

Your goals reveal what your intentions are, but your calendar shows what you are committed to.

Be as comprehensive as you can. Get it all out. This is real work, but it doesn't actually take very long when you have your calendar to hand.

If you put a timer on for five or ten minutes you could definitely have it done by then.

Against each entry, write the number of hours it takes. I suggest you then convert everything to a weekly equivalent (multiply the hours of daily activities by five, divide the hours of monthly activities by four and the hours of annual activities by fifty-two, for example).

Now score each activity from one to ten, with the proviso that you can't sit on the fence and use the number seven. Seriously. Seven is a 'meh' number that sounds quite good but is actually closer to five than to ten. So choose six or eight instead, which gives you the following options:

- » 1–3: 'RED' tasks that bore, drain or frustrate you. You probably aren't particularly competent in these tasks either, simply because they don't excite you.

- » 4–6: 'AMBER' tasks that you're fairly neutral about. You're probably good at them, but they don't inspire you and they're not the most valuable use of your unique skill set.

- » 8–10: 'GREEN' tasks that excite, fascinate and motivate you. They are high-value tasks you enjoy and they play to your unique strengths.

If you have a good mix of red, amber and green, your focus areas will be very clear. If everything is mainly one colour, perhaps see if you can 'recalibrate' to differentiate some more. The key thing is to develop insight about your use of time, and have a baseline to work from.

DEFINE YOUR STARTING POINT

COMMITMENT INVENTORY

Task	Frequency	Duration (hours)	How valuable & exciting is this activity (1–10)?	Hours per week equivalent
Weekly team call	Weekly	1	6	1
1:1s with direct reports	Weekly	6	8	6
All-hands meeting	Monthly	3	5	0.8
Email	Daily	2.5	2	12.5
Quaterly Business Review (prep and delivery)	Quarterly	40	6	3.3
Customer visits	Weekly	9	9	9
Diversity project meetings	Weekly	2	8	2
Various 1:1s with peers	Weekly	4	8	4
Industry conference	Yearly	16	6	0.3
Coaching session	Weekly	1	10	1
Speaking engagements	Yearly	40	6	0.8
Leadership team offsite (incl prep)	Quarterly	16	9	1.3
Leadership team meetings	Monthly	2	6	0.5
Thought leadership	Monthly	8	8	2
Technology refresh project meetings	Monthly	4	3	1
Ask me anything sessions	Monthly	1	3	0.3
Calendar management	Daily	0.5	1	2.5
Expenses & approvals	Weekly	2.5	1	2.5
Total				**50.8**
of which green		50%		25.3
of which amber		13%		6.7
of which red		37%		18.8

Make sure at the end of this activity that you know the following four numbers, which capture your current commitments:

1. The total number of 'committed hours per week', right now

2. How many of those hours are 'green' (energising and valuable)

3. How many of those hours are 'amber' (neutral)

4. How many of those hours are 'red' (draining and frustrating)

Enough reading. Now go ahead and do the work.

Build your Commitment Inventory.

> *You can find interactive tools to analyse your time commitments, along with the other resources for this book, at https://xquadrant.com/bookbonuses*

CHAPTER 11

Set the boundaries

Nature abhors a vacuum. Rising water floods the plain until it meets a wall.

In business and life, it's the same. Infinity floods in from all directions and it brings no boundaries of its own. It will swamp you until you erect a barrier yourself.

When I was at Cisco, I saw two or three colleagues burn out. One of them told me he couldn't cope with the constant calls to California that ended at midnight for him in Europe. The demands were too great, he said, and it was taking a toll.

The thing was, I had exactly the same role and finished no later than 7 p.m. And I was doing at least as well and having at least the same impact. The key difference was that I'd decided to work no later than 7 p.m. and he'd decided to work no later than midnight. He didn't see it that way; he saw himself as 'having to' be on these late calls. But even he had boundaries; he wasn't staying up until 4 a.m. for work calls. So the question was simply: where do we draw the line?

If you don't set the boundaries someone else will. So before defining your goal, decide what the important boundaries are for you.

At this point, fear can kick in. Our sense of identity can kick in. We're the person who sacrifices themselves for the team. We're worried we won't be able to get done everything we need to. We're concerned about what others will think. It's not practical. We 'need' to be at this meeting. We 'need' to always be checking our email. We're convinced that if we create boundaries then we'll fail at our objectives. It might work for others, but not for us.

Sometimes we just can't imagine life with boundaries. We're standing neck-deep in water on the floodplain, and can't imagine what life would be like if there was a dam just upriver. But once the barrier is there, there's new life and freedom and everything actually becomes so much easier.

I'm calling on you to be the powerful person you are. Creating boundaries is an act of leadership and of self-determination. It's a powerful step to creating your own future and freeing yourself up for strategic activity. It's an act of decisiveness. It takes some courage, but on the other side you will find freedom and – perhaps surprisingly – respect from the very people you feared would be upset at these new constraints.

> *Creating boundaries is an act of leadership and of self-determination. It's a powerful step into creating your own future and freeing yourself for strategic activity.*

A friend of mine declared on the first day of work at a major investment bank that he would be leaving at 6 p.m. and he didn't work on Sundays. This raised a few eyebrows to say the least, as it went against the prevailing culture. But by establishing his boundaries, and then delivering good work, he earned the respect of his colleagues and his working hours were simply integrated into the thousands of other constraints that every business has to operate within.

This is the key insight: there are already thousands of constraints and boundaries. The boss has a meeting; the customer needs the shipment by Monday; Julie is ill; Bob isn't very good at design work; the IT system is inefficient. If you decide to be the 'degree of freedom' and compensate for all these other constraints, you will drown in the waters of other people's convenience and you'll fail to make the contribution you are here to make. But if you keep your highest contribution at the front of mind, and you create boundaries to protect what's truly important, then the rest of the system will adapt to take that into account.

Remember, every 'yes' hides a 'no'. You say yes to your boss; you say no to your family. You say yes to your colleagues' low-level request, you say no to your most strategic project. You say yes to social media, you say no to writing your book. It's time to accept the responsibility and architect your life for impact.

Remember, every 'yes' hides a 'no'.

CREATE FORTS AND PRISONS

To create better boundaries, decide on your Forts and on your Prisons. These are two terms for certain sorts of time blocks that I learned from Shane Melaugh, the founder of Thrive Themes. Forts protect and keep things out; Prisons restrain and keep things in. Both create boundaries in your life.

MAKING TIME FOR STRATEGY

	Sun	Mon	Tue	Wed	Thu	Fri	Sat
		▲ FORT ▼		▲ FORT ▼			
		▶ PRISON ◀					

Here are a few examples of Forts and Prisons.

You might decide to create an hour of work on your top improvement project every Monday morning. Create a Fort, a blocked-off period of time in your calendar for this specific high-value activity.

You might decide to only process email at specific times of day. After all, no great life or business was built sitting in the mailroom! Create a Prison, a blocked-off slot in your calendar outside of which you don't look at email.

You decide to finally prioritise your family, and you create a Fort every evening for that.

You're fed up with the low-level admin tasks and create an Admin Prison – a ninety-minute sprint on a Friday morning to clear up the loose ends from the week.

Personally, I have one day each week where I have *no* meetings. It's a fantastic Fort in my week and allows me to make real progress on my strategic work.

Why not experiment with this? You could perhaps begin with one 'no-meeting morning'.

When it comes to putting this into practice, I have two conflicting pieces of advice for you. The first is to start tiny. Be incremental, gradually reshape your time, and go from win to win. And the second is to start bold. Make some decisive moves that dramatically reshape your week. You will know the best way for you.

What are the Forts and Prisons that you need to establish?

CHAPTER 12

Make the bold decisions

'We have to cut the workforce by thirty per cent,' said the founder with tears in his eyes.

It was 2001. The dot-com bubble had burst, and demand for his business's products had collapsed. He was pointing to a chart that showed the cash flow of the company and the fact that the business would be bankrupt in three months unless drastic action was taken.

Today that business turns over almost £100 million and is incredibly robust. But back then, taking that hard decision made the difference between life or death for the company. In a stroke, the cost base of the firm came back in line with the demand, and the business was healthy once again.

Indeed, a common refrain from leaders who've been through these painful processes is that 'it's better to cut quickly and deeply'. Rather than limp on for years making incremental improvements, it's often better to make some bold moves and quickly set the business on a healthy footing. The advantage of this is approach is that you quickly re-establish profitability, which allows you to start investing for the future.

The same thing applies on a personal level. Incremental progress is no way to beat infinity.

If you are drowning in operations, incremental moves will not give you the space you need to make big progress on the things that will determine your future success. Instead, you need to create Strategic Time, and fast.

> *Incremental progress is no way to beat infinity.*

Pull out your Commitment Inventory and have a look at those red and amber activities. Those are your prime targets. Those are the places where you are playing safe, thinking small, and where you are stuck in the tyranny of the incremental.

INTRODUCING THE CRASH METHOD

We're about to get incredibly practical. The CRASH™ method consists of five strategies that will allow you to quickly free up significant amounts of time. These strategies are:

- » Cut – Abandon or cancel the activity completely.

- » Reduce – Shrink the scope of the activity dramatically.

- » Assign – Delegate some or all of the activity.

- » Systematise – Build templates, scripts or processes to streamline.

- » Hold – Defer the activity to a future date.

THE CRASH METHOD

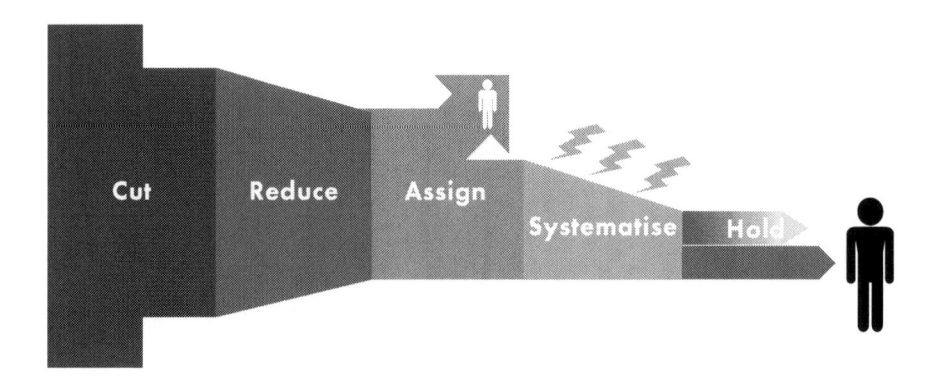

Cut — Reduce — Assign — Systematise — Hold

These five strategies get progressively weaker. It's more powerful to Cut than Hold, for example. However, they can be combined for great effect. For example, you can Reduce and Assign, or you can Assign and Systematise.

We'll explore each strategy in the upcoming chapters, but first two words of warning.

Firstly, the objective right now is to determine some very specific actions. Some of them you will be able to implement immediately. Some of these might require some conversations before you're able to make them happen. That's OK; we'll cover that in *'The Influence Challenge'* later in this book. For now, decide *what* has to happen. You can figure out exactly *how* to make it happen later.

Secondly, behind each of these strategies there's a deeper mindset challenge. As I mentioned earlier, the temptation is to make incremental adjustments: cancel one or two meetings, delegate a token task, and so on. But I want to encourage you to remember your high-value activities, focus on maximising your ultimate contribution to the organisation, and be bold in making your moves.

Go beyond safe. Aim high.

To do this, set yourself a bold intention before we begin. How about you decide to free up 20 per cent of your working week? In other words, make some decisions that will eliminate the least-productive quintile of your time and attention. You'll get a day back each week to invest in next-level activity!

Make yourself a promise about the time you will free up. Write it down. And let's begin.

> *You can find worksheets and interactive tools to help you implement the CRASH process, along with the other resources for this book, at https://xquadrant.com/bookbonuses*

CHAPTER 13

Step 1: Cut

No one can withstand the onslaught of infinity without powerful weapons. And the most powerful weapon is the sword of your will. Finely honed, it cuts away the extraneous, the superfluous, the incremental. It frees you from the net of past success and allows you to rise.

The strategy of 'Cut' is obvious, simple and powerful. It's so powerful it might just scare us as we realise that something so simple could be the key to our own freedom.

Cutting an activity is pure. It means to abandon or cancel the activity completely. It's based on a decision that the activity is no longer relevant, effective, desirable or necessary.

The 80/20 rule states that 20 per cent of our effort generates 80 per cent of our results. Put another way, the remaining 80 per cent of our effort generates just 20 per cent of those results. Of that 80 per cent of low-value activity, we can apply the 80/20 rule again and again, and after a few seconds on our calculator we discover that the least effective 20 per cent of our time contributes 0.001 per cent to our results! This is just a theoretical approximation of course, but the point is: the bottom 20 per cent needs cutting!

You may be feeling that you've done all the pruning you realistically can do. If that's the case, may I suggest you hand your calendar to a colleague and ask them to identify the least valuable 20 per cent of your time? In workshops, this approach has always resulted in the identification of low-value activities.

If you're still resistant to the idea that there are only a few incremental things you can cut, try these questions. If you were taken seriously ill and could only work half time, what would you keep, and what would you cut? And which tasks would somebody absolutely *nailing* your role have cut completely?

MAKE YOUR LIST

Let's get into action. Work your way through your Commitment Inventory and decide what you want to cut completely. Your list might include specific instances of the following:

- » Zombie meetings – those recurring appointments that used to have life and purpose, and now don't seem to achieve much.

- » Meetings where you don't make a unique and powerful contribution. If you need to stay in the loop, find a less time-consuming way to find out what happened. (This means most 'informational meetings' can go.)

- » Old responsibilities that don't align with your main area of accountability.

- » 'Ought to/Should do' projects that are on your list, but aren't actually getting done.

» All those hours you spend helping colleagues out with low-level requests that they should be going to other people for (or working out themselves).

» Those projects you're micromanaging. Trust your team.

» Superfluous review cycles. See above – trust your team.

» Pointless emails that clutter up your inbox. Unsubscribe. Filter.

» Pointless Slack channels that just add noise. Mute. Leave.

Karen is a marketing leader who participated on one of our *Impact Accelerator* programmes. She told me, 'It seems obvious really, but only attending meetings where I could add real value has been a game-changer. Before my days were crammed with meetings, but now I actually have space to get on with the work I really need to attend to.'

Remember, the sword is a powerful weapon. It will feel drastic if you are not used to saying 'no' and prioritising ruthlessly. Don't be shy in applying it: remember every 'no' you say now allows you to say 'yes' to what matters most. Let FOMO go and embrace JOMO (the joy of missing out). And remember that if you cut too hard (highly unlikely!) you can always reinstate things later.

The weapon is yours. Go use it.

Decide what elements of your Commitment Inventory you can Cut.

CHAPTER 14

Step 2: Reduce

You can free up whole swathes of time by the second strategy: reduce. Reducing is all about questioning the time requirements of your different commitments, and then shrinking those dramatically.

Who said that you needed to attend those project updates every single week? Or that a fifty-page presentation is really necessary for the quarterly business review?

When you reduce, you become a masterful alchemist. Like a skilled chemist or cook, you distill a diluted solution down into a powerful concentrate. You boil off the watery mass and are left with the strong and flavoursome essence. Suddenly, a little goes a long way.

Pull out your Commitment Inventory once again and look for creative ways to reduce the time required for each of your lower-scoring activities. Here are some angles you can try.

You can reduce scope. You can, for example, eliminate a work-stream from a project, or reduce the extent of the data your project will analyse.

You can reduce frequency. For example, make weekly meetings fortnightly or even monthly, decide to only attend one in every two or three meetings, or check your social media at a slower pace. Skip half of the all-hands calls and ask for a quick debrief from a colleague. Imagine the time you would free up if you could attend the meetings in your diary half as often!

You can reduce quantity. Deliver shorter, more succinct presentations or reports. Attend just the first thirty minutes of those two-hour meetings. Offer a single review, rather than requiring multiple review cycles.

You can reduce quality. You might agree to provide key comments rather than a fully reworked draft, or send through a photo of your handwritten notes rather than typing them up.

Once again, the 80/20 rule is your friend. Ask yourself, 'How can I achieve 80 per cent of the results with 20 per cent of the effort? What is the most valuable 20 per cent of this activity?'

The beauty of the Reduce strategy is even your highest-value activities (HVAs) can benefit from it. Within your HVAs, there's probably a core activity that's really generating the value. Can you double down just on that component, and reduce the effort spent on other parts of the task?

Remember that reducing the work an activity requires is a strong and positive move. We very often over-engineer tasks, and reducing quality in one area allows us to attend more closely to the higher-value activities that generate a bigger return on the time invested. You are simply modulating the time and effort involved in producing your 'deliverable' to reflect the importance of the activity in your overall list of priorities.

Finally, be bold. Experiment. Avoid incremental reductions that don't move the needle. Aim to cut at least one-third of the effort involved in any activity.

Decide what elements of your Commitment Inventory you can Reduce.

CHAPTER 15

Step 3: Assign

The third strategy in the CRASH process is Assign. This is where you delegate some or (preferably) all of an activity to someone else. However, as we know, delegation is easier said than done – so we need to decide what's going to be different this time.

Here are three reasons you're probably not delegating effectively, and what to do about that.

CLARIFY YOUR INTENT

First of all, you won't delegate much if your very first question is *how* you can delegate. Commit first of all to determining your intent. Very specifically, what activities and responsibilities *should* be assigned? Often we get stuck in the 'how hole', but the first stage is to make the internal decision that this is not an activity that we should be doing. Only at this point can you allow your mind to start to work on a different question – not 'should I delegate this?' but 'how should I delegate this?'

Delegation difficulties come from various sources, but they are mainly internal. For example, you might say to yourself, 'I'm good at this: do I want to give up something I know I can do well?' Or, 'Doing this has made me successful in the past – what happens if I stop doing it?' So it's important to focus on the future and ask yourself, 'Is this a high-value activity representing my next level of impact, or is it actually holding me back at this point?'

One of my clients discovered in a Commitment Inventory review that around 30 per cent of his time was used on three recurring business processes that he was personally responsible for. Earlier in his career he had benefitted greatly by taking ownership for these complex and ill-defined parts of the business. But in conversation, he suddenly realised that they were now sucking almost a third of his time and not adding extra value. He was simply spending much of his time 'keeping the lights on' and not solving the new challenges faced by the organisation.

My client had no idea how he would be able to assign these tasks to his team. His team were too junior, they weren't so skilled, he had no time to write documentation, the risks were too high… There seemed plenty of excuses and reasons not to move forward.

But he drew a line in the sand. 'I *will* delegate these tasks within the quarter,' he announced to me. He didn't know how, but he could see that his path of greatest contribution lay in other parts of the business.

Fast-forward three months, and it was done. When the motivation and clarity is there, finding solutions to the practical difficulties of handing tasks over turns out to be easier than we think.

DEFINE THE OUTCOME

The second barrier to delegation is that your thinking is sloppy. We often don't know exactly what we want (i.e. the ultimate result we are looking for) or how we ourselves are currently going about getting the thing done (i.e. our own methodology and decision-making process), so we can't explain it to others. Definition is the first step in delegation! It's the hard work and the high-value activity. What exactly does success look like, and what exactly are the key steps?

> *Definition is the first step in delegation! It's the hard work and the high-value activity. What exactly does success look like, and what exactly are the key steps?*

At one point in my career I led a team responsible for complex financial and economic analysis, working with industry experts to build business cases for large customers. As we looked to scale our impact and delegate parts of the process, we received real pushback. 'This is highly skilled and high-end professional activity. It requires years of experience and every situation is unique. We can't reduce this to an outsourceable process.' Well, actually we could and we did!

The secret was to figure out the mental process that the consulting team unconsciously went through on 80 per cent of the engagements. We were then able to identify specific elements of that process that could be defined, standardised and scaled. In fact, quality went up because the experts could spend more time on their unique expertise, and the discipline of thinking through the process meant that steps weren't missed or glossed over, creating more reliable deliverables. It was like moving from cottage industry to a production line – output increased dramatically (at least 40 per cent) and quality issues declined.

CREATIVELY FIND ASSIGNEES

The third barrier preventing you from delegating is that you might not be able to think of anyone to assign things to. Perhaps you have no team right now, or everyone is already flat out.

Well, the advent of virtual assistants and websites like fiverr.com or upwork.com means that delegation is more accessible and affordable than ever, even if you don't have a team or personal assistant. Also, if there really is a strong business rationale for delegating something, perhaps your first improvement project will involve securing the necessary funding to make that possible! Finally, perhaps you need to help your whole team free themselves up from their low-level tasks, by taking them through the CRASH methodology as well.

If you're in senior leadership and don't yet have an amazing personal assistant and/or chief of staff, then the most valuable advice I can give you (that will pay for the cost of this book a million times over!) is to do whatever it takes to hire one, as soon as possible. The right person in this kind of support role will act as a true multiplier, defending your diary, taking on tasks you shouldn't be doing, and helping you spend more and more time on your high-value activities. If you don't yet have this person in place, please stop reading this book right now, and take whatever tiny step you need in order to kick off that process.

WHAT ARE YOU GOING TO ASSIGN?

The time has come. Review your own Commitment Inventory and decide, for each item, whether you will assign some or all of the activity. Remember, you're making a decision of intent here. You don't need to know how exactly you'll do it.

STEP 3: ASSIGN

Here are some questions you can ask to direct your thinking.

- » Are there processes that someone else could, after an appropriate handover, take entire responsibility for?

- » Are there meetings that somebody else could represent the department at?

- » Are there recurring email threads that should be rerouted to a more appropriate person?

- » Are there complex tasks that you can't delegate right now in their entirety, but that have repetitive sub-activities that can be explained or documented once and then performed, at least in part, without supervision?

- » Are there decisions that you can empower others to be taking, perhaps within certain constraints and parameters that you can determine?

So, decide. Let it go. Assign it.

Decide what elements of your Commitment Inventory you can Assign.

CHAPTER 16

Step 4: Systematise

You've Cut, Reduced and Assigned. It looks like the things still on your list are going to stay with you for now. Now it's time to bring out the power tools. It's time to Systematise.

Systematising is all about reducing the mental overhead of the different activities on your plate, by harnessing better processes and better technology. Systematising has been described as 'delegating to the machine', but it's also about breaking down vaguely defined tasks into clearer steps and decision-points so that you don't have to make nuanced, complex decisions on a repetitive basis.

Look for repetitive activities where you can create templates, scripts or processes to make them faster and more efficient.

Don't get bogged down in designing or implementing the systems yet! Just identify where there is inefficiency and repetition in your activities. Go through your Commitment Inventory – and also think on a more granular level about the kinds of messages, calls and emails you regularly engage in.

Templates

Prepare templates for typical emails you regularly send. One handy hint is to save them as 'signatures' in your email program, or use an app like TextExpander or Typinator to summon them with just a few keystrokes. Similarly, use the short-code function on your mobile phone to make processing emails from your mobile vastly quicker.

This might seem like a minor gain, but you'll be amazed at how many almost identical sentences and even whole paragraphs you write each week: from 'Thanks for the message, but I'm not interested' or 'Putting you in touch with Alex, who manages my diary…' to 'I'm no longer responsible for questions related to sales operations; I recommend you reach out to John Smith about that' or 'The best thing would be for you to book a convenient slot using this booking link. If you have difficulties my assistant can help organise this manually.'

The advantage of preparing templates is twofold. Firstly, it's much faster. Secondly, it allows you to create better responses. You put real thought into the template, and the result is going to be better than a bunch of ad-hoc emails, quickly written in the moment. So start building a 'swipe file' of commonly used scripts and templates. I provide a few scripts later on in this book, and a much larger repertoire is available in the online bonus area.

Apps

There's an app for that! There are apps that make many aspects of our daily lives more streamlined. The obvious example is the scheduling app (like Calendly or Book Like A Boss). Rather than email back and forth you make it easy for people to grab time on your calendar. But there are many more. My current favourite is an app called Bridge that systematises the process of making introductions between people in your network. Get curious about productivity apps – they are tools that can make a huge difference.

Processes

Articulating your current processes and workflows allows you to get really specific about how you accomplish certain things, and opens up a question about whether you need to do every step in the process yourself.

For example, what's the process you go through to build the quarterly business review presentation? Chances are, quite a lot of that could be done by other people, but before you can systematise you do need to understand and articulate the process. This is why systematising is often a great first step towards assigning an activity to someone else.

Some major processes to think about include how you manage your email inbox and your messaging apps. We'll cover that later, but for now ask yourself: how systematised is my email and message processing?

Batching

It's been well-documented that context switching – moving from one task to another – takes considerable time and attention. This means it's better to batch activities together into blocks to make it easier to process multiple similar activities in one session. For example, process all invoices and payments once a week rather than on a daily basis. Do your expenses in one big session every week/month instead of a couple of expenses every day. Process email at specific moments in the day, rather than in a drip-fashion throughout the day.

STEP 4: SYSTEMATISE

Go ahead and identify the biggest opportunities to bring out the power tools and Systematise. Once that's done, we can turn to the final CRASH strategy, which is all about the power of procrastination.

Decide what elements of your Commitment Inventory you can Systematise.

CHAPTER 17

Step 5: Hold

I once had a boss who never said 'no', but still managed to keep his to-do list manageable.

Never saying 'no' isn't a strategy I'd recommend. Far better to be strong, confident and purposeful about the contribution you can best provide. However, we can all learn from my former boss's strategy.

He pushed things into the future. If someone asked him to take on something that wasn't a priority, he'd simply propose an extended timeline.

'We can work on that project, but we don't have capacity for another six weeks.'

'I'd love to present to your team, but won't be able to do that for two months.'

'We can get to that in a month, but if you want a faster turnaround I suggest you contact John in Operations.'

The strategy of Hold is the weakest of the five CRASH strategies. (Remember, the strategies get progressively weaker, from Cut to Hold.) However, it still packs a punch and absolutely needs to be a part of your toolkit.

STEP 5: HOLD

Holding is simply the art of pushing the activity into the future. This is 'managed procrastination', where you decide that the activity in question can be delayed for a few weeks until you have cleared bigger priorities. It's weaker than the other strategies because ultimately the work is still on your plate, but as we'll see it can and does create space in your calendar for more important things.

There are five ways this strategy works.

Firstly, as my boss found, saying 'yes but in the future' actually results in fewer commitments. Often if something can't be done immediately, people find another way to do it, or the need for that activity actually goes away of its own volition, such as when the company strategy changes, the market shifts, there's a new internal reorganisation, or a different priority emerges.

Secondly, you can use Hold to create an 'air bubble' in your calendar. Let's say you have a monthly call you feel you can't Cut, Reduce or Assign. Perhaps you could say 'I've got some big projects on right now, and won't be able to make the monthly call until February. Could you keep me updated via email in the meantime?' You've just pushed your next meeting out several months and given yourself some breathing space.

Thirdly, the very act of proposing an extended timeframe opens up a conversation about priorities and resources that can be helpful. If your boss piles things on, and you have difficulty saying no, proposing realistic timeframes can stimulate a discussion about priorities. 'We can get to that project once we've closed the Simmonds account at the end of the quarter. Or would you prefer we push the Simmonds work out two months?'

Fourthly, you can use Hold to delay your decisions about activities themselves. You can say, for example, 'We can't make any commitments about new projects until our operations meeting in a fortnight.'

Finally, putting something on Hold also allows you to test the real impact of Cutting, Reducing, Assigning or Systematising it. Consider Hold as an experiment; you can find out if there's really as much downside as you think to stepping out of an obligation. What if you were to experiment and pause some activities? For example, no social media posting for a month? No all-hands calls this quarter? No more weekly management update emails until February?

Applying the Hold strategy is simple. For each activity on your list, ask yourself: how much would it matter if I delayed this one, two or four weeks? One or two quarters? What would really change? Can I put the activity on pause, or extend deadlines?

Once again, at this stage you don't need to act on your decision; you just need to identify that various activities can be delayed, postponed or held for a certain period of time.

Decide what elements of your Commitment Inventory you can Hold.

CHAPTER 18

You've built a perfect system for being busy

The last few chapters have been squarely in the tactical necessities of cleaning up your Commitment Inventory and overall use of time. You've been building a practical roadmap to pinpoint exactly what needs to be eliminated from your calendar. You can think of it as a time-bound project, a sprint to make a meaningful dent in your low-value tasks.

Now we'll turn our attention to how you'll be able to preserve focus and maintain your streamlined calendar in the future. After all, going on a diet (even a CRASH diet!) to lose some weight is one thing, but changing your eating and exercise habits to keep the weight off is another.

Many years ago, a mentor of mine realised that he was making more money than he had ever made in his life, yet he still seemed to be struggling with finances. Recalling the words of *his* coach – 'the results you get are perfect for the system you have created' – he picked up a pen and sketched a mind map of how he was creating 'A Perfect System for a Constant Struggle Around Money (No Matter How Much You Earn)'.

Elements of this 'perfect system' included:

- » Don't look at my financial situation.
- » Don't try to understand the tax regime.
- » Buy unnecessary items whenever I'm feeling flush.
- » Have friends who think $100,000 is a lot of money.
- » Don't save.
- » Don't give.
- » Create just enough money to get by, then move into busywork.

As he sketched this system, he wryly realised that he was a *master* at struggling with money – no matter how much he earned. He was world class! He could teach this!

A friend of mine had a very different challenge. 'I only ever seem to date emotionally unavailable men,' she complained. Our coach shot back the same reply: 'The results you get are perfect for the system you have created.' He asked her to explain *her* perfect system. Out it came. Seeing coldness as a challenge. Feeling unworthy of genuine affection. Going against her gut instinct when she was invited on a date. And so it went on.

We have all built perfect systems for the results we are creating in our lives.

YOU ARE PERFECTLY BUSY!

You are perfectly busy. You have designed a perfect system to generate the precise amount of busyness that you are currently experiencing in your life.

YOU'VE BUILT A PERFECT SYSTEM FOR BEING BUSY

You might react against this idea. 'No, it's not my system: it's just the stage my company is going through.' 'It's just that several projects have come to a head.' 'You've never met my boss – she really piles things on. I don't really have a choice.'

I want to suggest that these are simply stories you're telling yourself, stories that are convenient because you can avoid taking personal responsibility for your current situation. It's so much easier to blame others and cast yourself in the role of the victim. But let's take the route of radical responsibility instead. We have all built a perfect system for generating our current level of busyness.

So what *is* your perfect system? Grab a sheet of paper and sketch it out! This is a fun exercise, but it will also help you think deeply about what's going on, and truly see the degree of influence you really do have on how you allocate your time.

For example, your Perfect System for Being Crazy-Busy might include things like:

» Think that being busy is a sign of my value.

» Boost my self-importance by regularly telling people how crazy-busy I am.

» Never schedule time for my high-value activities.

» Maintain a horrendously long to-do list that I can never get through.

» Make decisions my team should be making.

- » Insist I review my team's output, multiple times. Don't empower them and let them take the consequences for their own quality standards.

- » Never take time to go for a walk and *think*.

As you do this exercise, there are a couple of specific areas you might want to drill into, including messaging and meetings. Let's look at those in some more detail.

YOUR PERFECT SYSTEM FOR SPENDING HOURS IN YOUR INBOX

Part of your perfect system is a whole area around email and messaging. The average professional spends over ten hours per week checking email and checks every six minutes! Moreover Matt Plummer, in a *Harvard Business Review* article, found that correcting four issues saved over five and a half hours each week on average. We'll get to those in a second.

Before we go any further, know your numbers, like any good manager. So grab some paper and jot down answers to the following questions:

- » How many hours do you spend on email and messaging?

- » How often do you check your inbox?

- » How many read messages are in your inbox?

- » How many unread messages are in your inbox?

- » What percentage of your email time do you consider strategic, driving your top projects forward?

» What percentage of your email time is basically responding to random stuff and other people's agendas?

Now, what's the 'perfect system' that you've built for email and messaging? Here are some common elements of many executives' email systems:

» Don't schedule email – just do it whenever I get a few minutes.

» Get sucked in all the time by notifications, so I keep getting distracted from my high-value activities. (Over-checking and dealing with notifications wastes around one hour and forty minutes per week, according to HBR).

» Keep around 3,000 messages in my inbox, so whenever I have a few minutes I can just scan up and down that long list to find something to do (scanning huge inboxes wastes a full two hours per week, according to the research).

» Don't organise – keep emails to action right away in the same place as things I'm waiting on or things I might want to read or refer to in the future.

» Train my stakeholders to expect an instant response from me – keep the pressure on!

» Keep solving other people's problems instead of working on my own HVAs.

» Do everything manually – barely use filters/templates.

» Spend ages sorting things into folders (which, incredibly, wastes seventy-five minutes per week on average).

- » Deal with irrelevant emails (which wastes forty minutes per week on average!).

- » Don't bother learning time-saving keyboard shortcuts, filters or other features.

- » Don't trust my assistant enough to process my inbox for me.

YOUR PERFECT SYSTEM FOR MEETINGS

Ineffective meetings are the scourge of modern business life. According to the *Harvard Business Review*, employees spend on average sixty-two hours per month in meetings, a full half of which is estimated to be wasted. The consequence of bad meetings is that passive-aggressive behaviour starts to become the norm, creating terrible meeting cultures. People show up late, fiddle with gadgets, multi-task. This creates a vicious circle of worse meetings and worse behaviour.

It may feel that you 'have' to go to all sorts of meetings, and you might feel that you can't get out of many meetings in your diary. I want to offer the possibility that you have much more freedom and choice than you believe. What if you took full responsibility for making the biggest impact possible, and made the moves you needed to cut out the fluff and the distractions? What would it look like to be bold? What would it look like if you only attended meetings that matter?

You have a 'perfect system for getting stuck in too many boring and pointless meetings'. How does that work exactly? Here are some ideas:

- » Accept all calendar invitations I receive, until my diary is completely full. Let the meetings pile up and swamp my calendar. Be driven by FOMO!

- » Have no clear policy for accepting or declining meetings, or assigning them to someone else.

- » Have no constraints or boundaries. Be always available. Accept evening calls on a regular basis.

- » Accept so many internal meetings that I don't have enough time for important customer conversations.

- » Never review my meeting commitments that have stacked up, and never purge 'zombie meetings' that used to have life and purpose but have now become lifeless and energy-sucking.

- » Never negotiate an exit clause before joining a meeting, meaning I find myself stuck in pointless sessions. An exit clause could be as simple as 'I can join for the first half hour, but may need to drop at that point.'

- » Don't tell my assistant how to decide which meetings to accept and which to decline.

WHAT TO DO WITH YOUR PERFECT SYSTEM

All the points above are just examples; what's really interesting is what *you* come up with. Try to find at least fifteen or twenty points. When you feel you've got everything out, see if you can add a handful more. You may find that you start with the surface-level issues, but if you push yourself to come up with more options you'll begin to look a bit deeper. This is where the insight happens.

The temptation at this stage is to build a fifteen-step plan to deal with all the elements in your perfect system. But I want to suggest a different approach.

Look at it. Laugh at it. Take it lightly, and give yourself grace. Put it somewhere you'll see, and just let it sink in over time. This process of 'gentle reflection' may well be enough for you to catch yourself as you implement different parts of this system: 'Ah, here I go, unthinkingly accepting calendar invitations again!' From this awareness you can make some different choices, but there doesn't need to be any guilt or stress.

For now, it's time to get to work. Grab a pen and paper and see what you come up with.

Draw out your 'Perfect System for Being Crazy-Busy'.

CHAPTER 19

Your $100 hammer

'I hate home improvement projects,' said Christopher, a colleague of mine. I was wondering what the link was to the shiny new smartphone he'd just unwrapped. This was a brand new iPhone that had been released just a day or two earlier, back in the days when a new iPhone release was a big deal.

'So I try not to do these do-it-yourself projects. But once a year, there's something that I need to fix myself. I head down to the hardware store and buy a cheap two-dollar hammer imported from the Far East. It falls apart very quickly, but it gets the job done and I'll just buy a new one next year when I need to do another job.'

'But,' he continued, fondling the shiny slab of glass in his hand, 'if I were a carpenter I'd invest in the top-end hammer. The $100 one. The titanium version with a shock-absorbing grip. After all, it'd be the tool of my trade, so I'd want the very best.'

He turned to me. 'I'm a knowledge worker. I spend my days using technology to get my job done. So this,' he said, waving the phone at me, 'is my $100 hammer. It's the tool of my trade. That's why I have a triple screen monitor setup in my office. It's why I have the best computer, the best phone. And why I've mastered the advanced functionality of the apps that most of us don't bother to scratch the surface of.'

The relevance of all this is that it's worth taking some time to think about how efficient you are when it comes to the bread-and-butter necessities of managing tasks and managing communications. Perhaps it's time to upgrade the workflow you're using, and invest in your own '$100 hammer'.

TO-DO LIST FOR YOUR TO-DO LIST

It's not the purpose of this book to teach you task management techniques. There are many good books out there on that, and various useful systems exist, although the foundational text is probably *Getting Things Done: The Art of Stress-free Productivity* by David Allen.

However, it is worth pausing to reflect on whether your approach for managing and organising your various tasks is serving you at this moment of your leadership journey, and what upgrades you'd like to make. So here's a to-do list for your to-do list; some prompts to help you reflect on and upgrade your own task management workflow.

1. Capture everything. 'Capture' is the first step of the GTD system, and most productivity experts agree that keeping a bunch of open loops in your head is a recipe for stress, poor prioritisation, and ineffectiveness. *What's the most frictionless way you can get ideas and action items out of your mind and into written form for later processing?*

2. Maintain a list of responsibility areas. If you want to capture everything, maintain a high-level list of your main responsibilities to serve as prompts. You might be focused on moving forward your main projects and customer commitments, but are you moving forward your goals as regards team development or

staying abreast of industry trends? *What are the top ten responsibility areas that you need to monitor and progress?*

3. Distinguish between projects and next actions. If you're procrastinating on a task, the chances are it's too big and the immediate next step isn't clear enough. Create a Projects list, and a Next Actions list (with one next action per project). 'Upgrade IT system' or 'Organise office party' are multi-step projects, and need a specific next action such as 'ask Jim for a list of potential vendors' or 'agree a date for the office party during our next team call'. *Do you have a clear list of ongoing projects and a clear list of immediate next actions?*

4. Conduct a weekly review. If you don't update and reflect on your lists of projects and next actions very regularly, you won't have confidence in your personal task management system, and you'll go back to navigating by gut feel and by trying to keep everything in your head. *When in the week do you review, update and reprioritise your to-do list?*

5. Don't over-organise. David Allen recommends that if a particular task is going to take two minutes or less, then it's best just to do the thing then and there instead of putting it into a list. *Can you block out an hour and blast through all the loose ends?*

6. Lean into the resistance. What's the next action on your list that scares you the most? Begin with that – it's probably the most important and impactful. *What's the task you are most reluctant to start?*

7. Set yourself up for success, and identify the big wins. You know

there's an infinity of tasks available, so identify three 'most important tasks' (MITs) at the start of each day and declare the day a success once those have been done. Personally, I also identify three MITs for the week, and for the month. *What are your three most important tasks for tomorrow?*

8. Purge. During your weekly review, be honest about your capacity to get things done and have the courage to cross things off the list that keep getting rolled forward, week after week. They're just not going to get done. *Is your to-do list realistic, or do you need to take it through the CRASH process once again?*

YOUR COMMUNICATIONS WORKFLOW

Is your email and messaging systems and workflow really serving you?

It takes some thought to create a really effective way to process the infinity of demands pouring into your different inboxes (including your email inbox, your messaging apps, your corporate chat apps, and so on). So let's get started.

First of all identify your most common email and messaging scenarios. What are the main categories of communication you receive? I'll share some typical categories, but if you want to truly own this for yourself, you'll jot down your own framework. At a high level there are messages demanding *action*, messages that you may need to *track/follow up*, and messages offering *information*.

Do you distinguish and process these different sorts of messages differently? Which of these categories is currently draining your time and attention the most?

What are the main kinds of actionable messages you receive? What are the common scenarios? For example:

- » Your manager requires a response

- » A team member wants advice

- » A peer makes a request to you

- » A customer expresses interest

- » You receive a meeting request

Once you have those, focus in. Which of these scenarios do you want to put your attention on and improve?

Now let's dig into your messaging workflow. At a high level, there are three steps here. First, you CHECK to find out what delights have found their way into your inbox. Then you DECIDE what kind of action/response is required. Finally, you organise yourself to ACT in some way. Let's review this CHECK/DECIDE/ACT process in more detail.

CHECK: When do I check new messages?

Typical answers: When I'm bored. When a notification pops up on my screen (distracting me even if I'm in the middle of some deep work or an important conversation!). When I have a few seconds of downtime.

A better answer: In specific time slots ('Prisons') that I've allocated for this. I know that no great life or business was built from the post room, so I've turned off notifications and actually close down email and messaging when I'm focused on more important tasks.

DECIDE: How do I decide what kind of action is needed from me?

Typical answers: I scan repeatedly through my inbox until I spot something that's either easy, or urgent. Then I do that. Rinse and repeat.

A better answer: I categorise my messages into a few types. For example. Do Today, Do Later, Wait, Store. Everything else I delete.

ACT: How do I get myself organised to complete this action?

Typical answers: I just spend a lot of time scanning and processing emails. I also wait for reminders to nudge me into action. I write every message manually.

A better answer: If it requires a minute or less, I'll just reply and be done with it. Everything else I group into categories, using folders or tags. Anything that's reference material (and therefore doesn't require an action apart from perhaps reading it) is kept separately from messages that require action. Anything I can't do quite yet (because I'm waiting on someone else, or I'm in monitoring mode) is also kept separate from things I can actually work on today. I rely on scripts and templates to process common use cases.

QUICK WAYS TO START TAMING YOUR INBOX

As you rethink your messaging workflow, here are some tactical tips to help you on your way. These might sound minor, but I can personally guarantee each of these is a valuable and practical tactic.

1. Experiment with a notification fast. Turn off all pings and pop-ups on both phone and computer for a week. You'll not want to go back.

2. Declare email bankruptcy. Move all unread emails to an archive folder and start afresh. If anything is really urgent, you'll remember – or someone will remind you. Tell your colleagues, 'Unfortunately, I no longer have access to any emails from the last month. If you need something specifically from me, please resend your message.'

3. Update your out-of-office or signature to inform others about your new approach to email. *'In order to focus on some important projects, I'm adjusting my email habits. I will review your message by the end of the week. If your message is urgent, then please call me.'*

4. Unsubscribe from any email list generating >X emails per week.

5. Use a different email address for informational email lists. In Gmail or Google Workspace, if your email is youremail@gmail.com then you'll also receive messages sent to youremail+anything@gmail.com – which makes incoming messages easy to filter away.

6. Use a text replacement service to make frequently used phrases and paragraphs instantaneous. Here are some to consider: 'What would you recommend?' 'Please let me know the options you've considered and which you think is the best way forward.' 'The best thing would be for you to book a convenient slot using this link.' 'Due to heavy workload I can't give you a personalised response to that for a couple of weeks. Here's our FAQ.'

7. Set up tags, labels or folders to distinguish messages that require different sorts of action over different timeframes. I'd suggest: Do Today, Do This Week, Do Later, Read/Review, Wait, Archive.

8. For a week, every time you see an email come in from any sort of email list, set up a filter to automatically move similar messages out of your inbox and into a separate folder. This means that very soon the only emails that are in your inbox are those that have been sent directly to you. All the subscriptions, bills, social media updates and newsletters are now out of sight and available for review as a batch, whenever you decide. Result: massively improved attention.

How can you upgrade your task management and communications workflows so that they become your '$100 hammer'?

CHAPTER 20

Three minutes, not thirty minutes

I cut his goal by 90 per cent, so that his performance would soar.

We'd just finished a coaching session, and Elliott was inspired. 'This is amazing! I'm going to work on this for thirty minutes every morning, first thing.'

My reply? 'Make it three minutes.'

You see, *tiny is transformational*. Let me explain why.

The power of tiny really came to life for me in the book *Tiny Habits* by BJ Fogg. Behaviour change is a product of our motivation, our ability, and the prompt that will cause us to act. When motivation is high, and there's a clear prompt to act, we can take on incredibly difficult challenges and succeed. But when motivation is low the task will need to be correspondingly easy if we are to actually complete it.

The problem is that we fail to realise that our motivation is fickle. It fluctuates wildly and will let us down at just the wrong time. In our moment of inspiration, when we set goals for ourself, we think *go big or go home*. Our pride kicks in, and we feel that we should be mature enough and powerful enough to put some big goals out there that require heroic effort to make happen. So we set ourselves a big challenge, like creating an extra thirty minutes in our day.

This is the path to failure. We start well, then life gets in the way and we break our own commitment to ourself. This leads in turn to a sense of guilt and powerlessness. But there's nothing wrong with us – we just haven't understood that motivation is fickle and that it's a poor foundation on which to build any kind of sustainable behaviour.

Instead, make it small. Make it easy. Focus on building one tiny habit, and build on that.

That's why I asked Elliott to spend three minutes on his project, not thirty. Anyone can find three minutes in a day. When he completed his three minutes, he was entitled to declare that a 'win' for the day and feel good about his progress. He was also allowed (but not obliged) to keep going... so some days he did ten, twenty, thirty, sixty minutes on his big project.

He'd created a game he could win. And when you're winning, you want to keep playing.

TINY MOVES YOU FORWARD

Tiny is great for habits. It's also great for anything important you're procrastinating on, because tiny actions are more concrete and less daunting than the larger, more amorphous and more intimidating projects we tend to avoid.

THREE MINUTES, NOT THIRTY MINUTES

I'm not a big fan of home improvement projects, and I can procrastinate on do-it-yourself tasks. So when I had to install some window blinds one Saturday morning, and could feel myself resisting, I gave myself a three-minute challenge: just put the blinds and the necessary tools in the appropriate room. I told myself at this point I could declare victory, as 'phase one' of the blinds project would be complete.

So I spent three minutes carrying the ladder, the toolbox, and the blinds up the stairs to the room in question. Success! However, I suddenly thought: 'I'm feeling good about this and I've got everything I need right here, so why not just spend a few minutes more screwing in the fittings and the job will be done?'

The blinds were installed half an hour later.

It's important to note I wasn't trying to trick myself here. Getting the equipment into the right room was already a victory, and I would have felt fine if I'd left it there for the day. But the power of 'tiny successes' kicked in, and accelerated my progress.

What is the tiniest commitment that you can make to increase the amount of Strategic Time you have available?

What's one three-minute habit you can build, to start moving you forward?

CHAPTER 21

Now, do the work

The last few chapters represent a simple, comprehensive action plan to dramatically shift your use of time now and in the future. There's a real temptation when reading a book to keep ploughing on, but I want to encourage you to stop at this point. Do the work. Get crystal clear on what a meaningful improvement of your use of time will look like, and build a simple plan to get there.

You've faced the fact that there is no Perfect Day, and that it won't get quieter next quarter. So today is the day for action, and you have all the steps you need.

You've built your 'Commitment Inventory' to actually understand your starting point. You know how many hours in the week are committed to your different areas, and you've assessed the value and motivation that each activity generates.

You've then started to design a new working life, by setting the boundary conditions, your non-negotiables, the frame within everything else is going to fit. Specifically, you've started to put Forts and Prisons on your calendar.

And then you've set a goal, a bold intention. How many hours do you actually want to free up for more important things? Now you have a game you can win.

With the goal in mind, you've applied the CRASH methodology to your Commitment Inventory in order to get you from your starting point to your desired end point. You should now know the specific moves you want to make – for example, the meetings to Cut, the deliverables to Reduce, the tasks to Assign, the processes to Systematise, and the projects to Hold.

And then you've turned your attention to understanding and redesigning those current workflows that got you into this situation in the first place: your Perfect System for Being Crazy-Busy.

Now, do the work by going slowly. Patiently take tiny steps and build sustainable habits that grow and compound over time.

However, building a plan isn't enough. To make this happen, you'll need to bring your stakeholders on board, so these changes are supported and welcomed by your superiors, your reports, and your peers. This is what we'll cover in Part 3, *'The Influence Challenge'*.

Alternatively, you can choose your own adventure by heading back to page 28 and deciding what your next priority area needs to be – or head back over to the online questionnaire to get a personalised recommendation about which part to focus on next.

Do you have a clear, simple plan to free yourself up for more strategic activity? If not, what else needs to get done? Go ahead

and block out time in your diary for those remaining activities, so you know you'll actually accomplish them.

> *Remember to check out the bonus tools available at https://xquadrant.com/bookbonuses/ that help you to quickly build your action plan.*

Part 3

THE INFLUENCE CHALLENGE

CHAPTER 22

The diet saboteurs

Jumping in to execution would be a mistake.

You've figured out a plan to extract yourself from lower-value activities, perhaps by working through the previous part of this book. But there's one essential step to take before you start to implement your plan.

Let's step out of the world of work for a moment, and think about what happens when you decide to eat more healthily or start a new exercise regimen. The people you are hoping will be your very biggest supporters – the people you live with – often turn out to be less than excited about your new commitment. Perhaps it disturbs their own schedule, or it might impinge on their own habits, or simply make them feel guilty for not taking on a similar discipline.

Whatever the reason, it's quite common to encounter resistance. Perhaps you'll hear that 'you could've found a more convenient time for your new exercise obsession' as you head out for your morning jog. Perhaps you'll get groans as you decline desert – 'come on, I baked it fresh today!' Or perhaps you'll be told to lighten up as you pass on the alcohol.

It's the people closest to you who are most likely to sabotage your efforts to improve. And without your family on board, it's incredibly difficult to make these kinds of lifestyle changes and build new habits.

It's the same thing in business. You are about to embark on a behaviour change. You'll be Cutting, Reducing, Assigning, Systematising and Holding various tasks, meetings and projects. You'll be creating Strategic Time and focusing on high-value activities and your top improvement project. But you exist within the complex interlocking organisational system of the business, and if you don't get your stakeholders on board, then you'll very quickly be pulled back to the status quo of everyone's current expectations of you.

> *If you don't get your stakeholders on board then you'll very quickly be pulled back to the status quo of everyone's current expectations of you.*

This is why it's important to slow down a little and create explicit agreements with your stakeholders. Sometimes this will look like you're simply informing people of a new way of working, other times it will look like more of a request, and sometimes it will be more of a negotiation.

It's tempting to shy away from these conversations, as it can feel uncomfortable explaining to someone why you will be reprioritising and spending less time on something. But this is the Influence Challenge that you need to embrace. Strategic Time – and breakthrough results – lie on the other side, because you'll have created a situation where other people's expectations are now pulling you forward into your preferred future, instead of dragging you back into lower-value tasks.

WHAT CONVERSATIONS NEED TO HAPPEN?

At this point, it's over to you. It's time to get specific. For each activity that you need to extract yourself from, decide what conversations need to happen, and with whom.

There are three main categories of conversation.

Firstly, there are *upwards* conversations (with your superiors). This is where you secure agreement for any moves that might impact them or the broader organisation, and you acquire some level of 'air cover' as you push forward with changes. For example, you might need to secure their agreement that you'll be unreachable on Mondays before 11 a.m. because you'll be working on strategic issues, or that you will only be attending the management review every second month going forward. You have less direct power in these conversations, but you can exert influence by showing how your proposals will ultimately benefit them.

Secondly, there are *sideways* conversations (with your peers). For example, you might need to speak with the Head of Product to renegotiate how their team interacts with your development team. Here the balance of power is distributed. You can simply announce some changes to them whilst collaborating and problem-solving together on other parts of your CRASH plan.

Finally, there are *downwards* conversations (with your reports). For example, you might assign a new task to them, hold them accountable to higher standards (so you don't need to redo their work), or ask them to attend a specific meeting in your place. Here you can be more assertive, but you'll still want to solicit their input and advice and create alignment and ownership.

The conversations are best done in order. Once you have your boss's buy-in, it's easier to go to peers, and once they are in alignment then you can move to your team.

List out the key conversations that need to happen for you to feel confident in making Strategic Time a reality.

> *You can find worksheets to help you map out your key stakeholder conversations, along with the other resources for this book, at https://xquadrant.com/bookbonuses*

CHAPTER 23

Preparing for high-value conversations

You've identified the critical conversations that will allow you to secure support for the changes you want to make to your schedule and responsibilities. Now it's time to prepare and give yourself the greatest possible chance of nailing these discussions.

Here's a roadmap for these high-value stakeholder conversations. It has four parts: context, proposal, questions, and agreement.

Context

Context frames content. In any conversation, the context of what we are saying is incredibly important, because it provides the filter through which we interpret the information coming to us. Even a simple phrase such as 'do you want any dinner?' could be a warm invitation, a word of caution, or an outright threat depending on the context.

So, begin your conversation with context. Why is this an important conversation to have right now, and where are you coming from? I find it helpful to speak to external factors (the organisational goals and pressures that have triggered this discussion), your personal motivation (why this conversation is important to you), and the benefits that you can see for the other person (or, at the very least, the fact that you want to minimise the negative impact on them).

FRAME WITH CONTEXT

CONTEXT

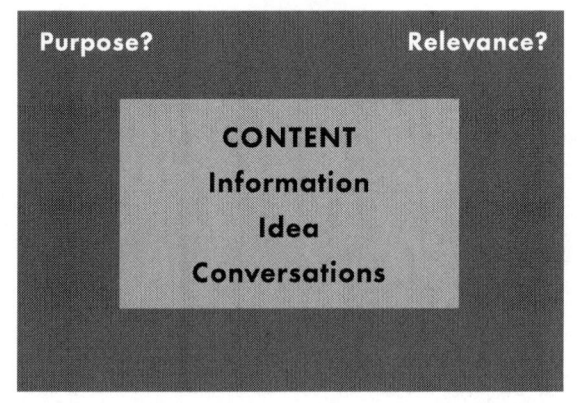

Purpose? **Relevance?**

CONTENT
Information
Idea
Conversations

For example, let's imagine that you've decided to implement an email policy, whereby you only process your inbox every two days and where you stop providing ad-hoc answers to requests that should properly be dealt with by your team. And you decide to speak to a peer about this.

The context part of your conversation might go as follows. 'I'm on point for a couple of really important projects right now and I'm finding email is really proving a distraction. I do want to support you and your team, but I need to make some changes so it works for both of us.'

At this point, you've established a trigger for the conversation (the new projects), you've reiterated your desire for partnership, and you've made it clear that change is essential.

Proposal

After the context, pause. This is a conversation, after all, and not a monologue! The other person might want to say something. When the time is right, move on to your proposal. Here I find less is more: state what you'd like to happen, what you need from them, what they can expect from you, and the benefits to both parties.

Remember to make the proposal as much about them as it is about you, especially if you don't have direct power to dictate the final outcome. In other words, try to give them a 'win' – either a practical benefit or an emotional payoff for accepting your proposal. Don't slip into too much detail or into self-justification. If they have questions they can ask later.

In our example above you might say, 'Right now I'm checking emails pretty much constantly, which is a recipe for lack of focus. Going forward I'm committing to processing my inbox every couple of days, so don't be surprised if it takes longer than usual to get back to you. I also realise I've been spending lots of time answering questions that my direct reports are better placed to deal with, so please would you check out our new FAQ page before contacting the team. If that doesn't answer your questions please email Jill with any questions related to Reporting from now on.'

Questions

Finally, open up the discussion. Depending on the context you might ask, 'Do you have any concerns about this?' or 'Do you see any issues with this from your side?' or perhaps a firmer, 'Is that clear?'

In this part of the discussion you are looking to build an explicit agreement about how things will work from now on. If the person has concerns they need to be able to express them: you can either reject or push back on these, explain how you can address their concerns, or adapt your proposal to take them into account.

For example, 'I get that sometimes things can't wait. If you absolutely need a response from me urgently, give me a call. Does that work?'

The balance of power in this discussion will vary depending on to whom you are speaking. You might have to negotiate more delicately with your boss than with a peer, and you might decide to simply inform your team about your new policy. I'd advise against extremes: there will be more buy-in from your team if you let them shape your ideas, and if you fail to push back against your boss's more unreasonable suggestions then you may fail to make significant progress.

If you are finding your counterpart to be somewhat intransigent, explain the benefits to them of your increased focus and productivity and be creative in finding solutions that give them what they need without undermining your ability to contribute at your highest level. Alternatively, shift your energy, and move from 'sales mode' to 'curiosity mode', asking them how they would solve the dilemma in a way that's mutually satisfactory. Get them proposing the solutions!

Agreement

Finally, ask for agreement. You can do this how you see fit. For example, you can quickly check they're OK to move forward on the basis you've just discussed, you can write it down and ask them to confirm they have the same understanding, you can ask them to tell you what they've understood from the conversation or confirm what the plan is going forward. The point is to make sure that each person explicitly gives their consent to the new working agreement. They might be doing some things differently, but you too might have agreed to provide different sorts of support to them.

The agreement means you've now got the green light to implement your CRASH strategy. Your counterpart is on board, and both sides have committed to it.

Take one high-value conversation you'd like to have and map out your key points, especially around the context and your proposal.

CHAPTER 24

Scripts

Let's get highly tactical for a minute. Here are some scripts you can use as jumping-off points for key stakeholder discussions. **For the sake of space, I've included just a few here, but you can download a full set as part of the book bonuses at https://xquadrant.com/bookbonuses/**

When you've been invited to a meeting that seems pointless

Hi (name),

Thanks for the invitation to (meeting name). I'm having to prune my attendance in meetings right back at the moment due to some high-priority projects, so can you please help me understand what you're looking to achieve and what you want from me?

1. What's the exact topic, and what's the agenda?
2. What decision needs to be made at the meeting?
3. What specific input do you need from me or my team?

Look forwarding to hearing from you.

When your manager asks for something but you are already overwhelmed with other projects

Hi (name),

Thanks for the clear instructions, which are much appreciated. However, it would be great for us to align around priorities as I'm already maxed out and will need to make some trade-offs.

Right now, as we discussed, my top priority projects are:

1. (project)
2. (project)
3. (project)

My preference at this point would be to maintain momentum and keep my focus on those, which would mean revisiting this new project later.

Alternatively, would you rather de-prioritise one of these in favour of this new project?

Thanks for clarifying.

When your manager asks for something that seems pointless, redundant, or unnecessary

Hi (name),

Thanks for your message.

At our last meeting, we decided that our goals right now are to (describe goals), with an overall focus on (describe big focus). Whilst this project could help us (explain new project goal), I'm wondering if it aligns with these bigger goals right now.

Do you think we can revisit this idea once we're further ahead on our top priorities? I just want to make sure I'm investing my time on the most important areas.

Let me know.

When you're asked to work on something that's not part of your job

Hi (name),

Thanks for your note. This project looks interesting but it falls outside of my core skill set and I'm under a lot of pressure to focus on my main business goals right now, such as (examples).

It sounds like an ideal assignment for (name of other person or team). They generally handle projects like this.

Can I suggest you try them?

Download the full set of scripts as part of the book bonuses at https://xquadrant.com/bookbonuses/

CHAPTER 25

Daddy speaks English

Systems fall into their lowest-energy configurations. Which is a fancy way of saying we all tend to take the easiest route, and settle there. You can see this effect every time someone says, 'It's easier to do it myself, so I'll go ahead and do just that.' You can see it every time a piece of work is passed to the experienced colleague who won't need handholding (instead of the junior colleague who will need support). You can see it every time an apple falls to the ground.

The important consequence of this is that you can actually change the overall outcome of a system (of interrelated people or things) just by inserting an 'energy barrier'. Sounds conceptual? Let's look at an example.

My family is binational; my wife was born French and I was born British. So when our kids were born we wanted them to learn both languages natively. The problem: we lived in France, and I was at home far less than my wife, meaning that their first few words were French, and they would start to talk to me in the language of Molière.

'Bonjour, Papa,' they might say. At this point I had a choice. If I defaulted to the easy option of just replying to them, the habit of speaking to me in French would become even more ingrained, leaving them fewer opportunities to speak and master English.

To shift the dynamics, I would insert an energy barrier. '"Bonjour, Papa" is French, isn't it? Daddy speaks English. How do you say that in English? Can you remember…? It's "Hello, Daddy". Can you say "Hello, Daddy" for me?'

Basically I made it so time-consuming to try to speak to me in French that they quickly switched into English when conversing with me… because it was so much easier! I'd successfully altered the end-state of this particular system by inserting an energy barrier to chatting with Daddy in French.

The same happens in business, which is a complex system with many drivers, players and constraints. Like any system, it will settle into its lowest-energy configuration. It will use the flexibility and degrees of freedom that it does have to work around the many constraints and limitations it faces. The question is: what constraints, boundaries and energy barriers of your own will you add into the system, or will you become the 'adjustment factor' that's basically the easiest way for everyone else to get their way?

> *The question is: what constraints, boundaries and energy barriers of your own will you add into the system, or will you become the 'adjusting factor'?*

As I mentioned earlier, a friend of mine announced, on his first day in his job at a major international bank, that he typically left at 6 p.m. and never worked Sundays… both eyebrow-raising constraints in that particular corporate culture. There was some pushback but he maintained his line and explained that he was perfectly able to get his job done within those constraints. Almost immediately, the system adjusted to this new constraint and he was indeed able to have a successful career in the firm.

Working in a global company poses various challenges, time zones being a clear difficulty. Some people set very clear boundaries for when they are available for calls, whereas other people habitually find themselves in conference calls in the middle of the night or at other unsociable hours. What is interesting is that people can succeed with both approaches: the question is simply whether you are bold enough to create some energy barriers (for example, making it clear what times you are available) that will force the system to readjust.

Energy barriers matter because they change the system in which you operate, and thereby create space for you to focus on your most strategic activities. You'll probably need to think about the energy barriers you have about accepting meetings, accepting projects and tasks, and around the discussions you have with your team. We'll cover these topics in the next chapters.

Where have you become the 'adjustment factor' in the systems, processes and relationships around you?

CHAPTER 26

You're a leader, not Sherlock Holmes

'Hey, boss, we need to speak.'

And so begins a text-message thread, which escalates into a phone call, which ends up taking half an hour or more of your day. You resolve the issue, but you're left feeling frustrated. It's just one more example of being dragged into a debate you really didn't want to spend that amount of time on.

If you dissect these conversations you'll probably find the world has turned upside down. You, the senior party, have had to play Sherlock Holmes, doing all the detective work to extract from your team member the clues to a solution to whatever case they've brought you. What's the issue, exactly? What are the pertinent facts? What options have been assessed? What's been tried? What's the current sticking point?

You're a good problem solver, so you're able to get to a conclusion of course, but it just takes so much time and attention. And the world is upside down because you're doing the hard work whilst your direct report just supplies inputs to your thinking process as you request them.

Welcome to a classic case of 'systems fall into their lowest-energy configurations'. Using the analogy from the previous chapter, you've taught your team how to speak to you in the wrong language!

In this case, your direct report has learned (probably through repeated experience) that if he or she comes to you with a problem like this, you'll willingly solve it for them. It's quick and easy for them; it absolves them of responsibility for the decision and it requires very little effort – just a quick phone call to you.

ASK FOR FULLY FORMED REQUESTS

To avoid this dynamic, which is unproductive for you and creates an unhelpful passivity in your team, it's time to raise energy barriers and make your team come to you with 'fully formed requests'. This means that they've done their homework before escalating to you. I recommend using the following outline, which helpfully contracts to the acronym SCARS, to guide the conversation.

S – Situation

In a sentence, what's the question we're trying to answer in this conversation? This makes sure that the discussion has a clear target outcome.

C – Context

Briefly, what are the salient facts? What chain of events has led us to this moment? You don't want a rambling monologue, you want the equivalent of 3–5 bullet points outlining the key facts.

A – Analysis

How have we assessed the issues? What options have we analysed? Here you are checking your team member has done the necessary thinking *before* coming to you.

R – Recommendations

What are 2–3 good ways forward, and of these which do you prefer? The advantage of having a couple of 'good ways forward' is that it avoids all-or-nothing thinking, encourages creativity and lateral thinking, and gives you some flexibility in choosing between options that your team have developed (instead of inventing a new option, which they won't have the same level of buy-in to). And the advantage of asking for their preferred recommendation is that it forces them to take a stance, rather than take the easy route out and defer to you.

S – Stakeholders

Who else needs to buy in before this decision can work, and have you spoken with them? The point here is to make sure that you're not being used as leverage in turf wars. Often people will come to their manager asking for an agreement on something, so they can go back to their peers and say 'the boss said we need to do this'. But you don't want to become the arbiter and referee between members of your team; you want them to come up with a common solution to their challenges. Asking the 'stakeholders' question allows you to check whether this is a solution being brought to you by all interested parties, or just by one faction of a bigger debate.

PUTTING SCARS INTO PRACTICE

Putting all this together, an example of a 'fully formed request' using the SCARS framework might look like the following:

'We need to decide what we're doing about the Vienna office, because one of the offers is expiring next week (Situation). If you remember, we have a choice of the serviced office by the airport, the historic building downtown, or the co-working space slightly further out (Context). The serviced office will be the cheapest of the three options by at least 30 per cent. Given we're projecting 25 per cent annual headcount growth, the co-working space will rapidly get expensive and we know the downtown building is already 35 per cent more costly than the airport location (Analysis). However, given staff preference is downtown, and our two biggest accounts are nearby, I do recommend that option as our final choice. Just one more contract from one of those clients will pay for the difference, and given the costs of attracting and retaining staff these days let's go for the more prestigious option. If that's too costly, I'd recommend the co-working space as a compromise option (Recommendations). I did check with operations and with the country manager, and they're both on board (Stakeholders). Are you OK with that?'

There are two ways to use SCARS. The first way is as a mental map for guiding these conversations when they occur. You can simply ask them to tell you the situation, the salient facts regarding the context, their assessment of the options, what they would recommend, and which stakeholders have bought in.

However, the best way is to teach your team that from now on you expect them to come to you ready to present any decision or discussion in SCARS format. Let them know you'll send them packing if they're not adequately prepared. You'll need to demonstrate leadership and follow through on this by raising the energy barriers and pushing back whenever people try to engage you without using SCARS:

'Hi, boss, can I get your input on something?'

'Sure. Email me your SCARS and once I've read it we can speak.'

'Hi, boss, can I pick your brains?'

'Are you ready to take me through your SCARS thinking?'

The goal is to get them to anticipate your reaction. Work towards getting to the following situation. It'll be a game-changer in terms of the level of distractions you have to deal with.

'Hi, boss, we need to speak about the Oxford situation.'

'You know what I'm going to ask for, right?'

'SCARS. Yes, I know. I'm ready.'

WHAT DO YOU RECOMMEND?

For smaller issues, SCARS might be overkill. A quick energy barrier, the response 'what do you recommend?', can work wonders on simple questions from your team.

'Hey, boss, should we go for the green or the yellow version of the graphic?'

'What do you recommend?'

'Hey, boss, is it time to follow up with XYZ Corp yet?'

'What do you recommend?'

'Do you think we should leave at 8.00 or 8.30 for the away-day?'

'What do you recommend?'

And then, once they give their recommendation, the reply, 'I'm happy to go with your recommendation' is normally enough.

SHIFTING BEHAVIOUR

Asking for fully formed requests (using SCARS), or simply pushing back on questions of minor detail (with 'what do you recommend?') are just two examples of raising energy barriers as a way to shift the behaviour of those around you. As people learn that you won't engage with them without a fully formed request, they'll become more prepared and they'll make much better use of your time. Rather than a forty-five-minute call for both of you, they'll spend fifteen minutes getting clear on the SCARS and perhaps emailing you the key facts, and you'll spend perhaps 5–10 minutes asking any other clarifying questions and then ratifying or modifying their proposed solution.

What's the next opportunity you'll have to apply the SCARS technique?

> Download the SCARS template and worksheet as part of the book bonuses at https://xquadrant.com/bookbonuses/

CHAPTER 27

The 'Accept' button is the lazy option

Many managers' diaries are overrun with meetings. Corporate shared calendars and automated scheduling systems contribute to this: people can often see your availability and it's easy to pop a meeting into any free slot. Furthermore, inviting people to a meeting is a low energy, low cost activity. It's as easy as adding an email address to a message, so meetings often have far more invitees than strictly necessary.

The result of this is a whole bunch of low-value meetings that crowd our diaries. Hopefully you've processed your existing meeting commitments using the CRASH framework, and you're down to just the high-value ones, but how do you protect your diary against meeting bloat as new incoming requests come your way?

This is where it's essential to raise energy barriers.

First of all, don't accept all the meeting requests you receive. The Accept button is the lazy option, the path of least resistance, but not the path of thoughtful and high-impact leadership. Unless you are fully convinced of your need to be there, use the Tentative button to signify that you've received the invitation but you're not fully convinced.

THE 'ACCEPT' BUTTON IS THE LAZY OPTION

The Accept button is the lazy option, the path of least resistance, but not the path of thoughtful and high-impact leadership.

Follow this with a message asking for more details. I recommend covering the five points I outline below, which can be summarised with the acronym TRADE.

» T – Topic: What is the exact topic?

» R – Running Order: What is the agenda, timing, location, duration?

» A – Attendees: Who else will be in attendance?

» D – Decision: What decision needs to be made at the meeting?

» E – Expectation: Why, specifically, do you need me to be there?

One client came up with his own one-line question: 'What unique contribution do you need me to make at this meeting that nobody on my team can provide?' Another: 'Can this meeting start without me?'

Once you have the response to your qualifying questions, you can decide: is the *meeting* necessary and are *you* necessary? Based on that, you can either accept, decline, or propose alternative solutions. There are various alternatives you can offer. You might suggest one of your team attend in your place; or that you skip this meeting but attend the subsequent one; or that you join for just the first thirty minutes; or that the organiser drops you a quick summary email with the main decisions and outputs.

Over to you. What are the specific questions you want to ask to qualify each meeting request? Decide on them, communicate them, and rigorously use them. You'll create a small energy barrier that will keep low-value meetings out of your diary and make the meetings you do attend more meaningful, relevant and productive.

At this point, why not go ahead and create a standard template you can copy and paste every time you receive an unqualified meeting invitation, asking for answers to these questions before you accept? It's a quick and simple way to create an energy barrier. You just need to be disciplined in enforcing it. You can find an example script for this in the online bonuses area for this book.

If people can't be bothered to answer these very reasonable questions, then embrace JOMO (the joy of missing out), skip the meeting, and get on with your important work instead.

How will you qualify each incoming meeting request?

CHAPTER 28

The magic of success checklists

David Marquet is a former US Navy captain who at one point unknowingly gave an impossible order, and his crew tried to follow it anyway. When he asked why, the answer was: 'Because you told me to.' His book *Turn the Ship Around!* chronicles how he turned his submarine from worst to first in the fleet by challenging the US Navy's traditional leader-follower approach.

One key insight from that book is that you can specify your desired outcome (what you want), or you can specify your desired process (how it's done), but you can't specify both.

THE VIDEO CAMERA TEST

When it comes to assigning and delegating tasks, most leaders fail to build a crystal-clear shared understanding of what a successful outcome truly looks like. So the person taking on the task is destined for failure, and you as the manager are destined for a frustrating cycle of iteration and explanation until the final result gets close to what you were hoping for.

> *You can specify your desired outcome,*
> *or you can specify your desired process,*
> *but you can't specify both.*

Here's how to do it. Find one task that you need to assign to someone. And now imagine that you go on holiday, and whilst you're on the beach sipping your Piña Colada, you get an email – not from the colleague to whom you delegated the matter, but from me.

In this email, I explain I've been doing some snooping. 'I took my video camera and broke into your offices. I stalked a few customers and recorded their conversations. I hacked into your IT system and read all the emails and messages about this project. And this is what I found out about the state of your project.'

In this email, I then go on to describe a few pertinent facts about the work that you delegated. I give you just a few bullet points outlining what I observed, telling you what progress has been made.

You read the email, and a big smile crosses your face. 'Perfect! That task is done. I don't need to hear any more about it.' And so you turn your phone off and roll over to tan your other side.

The big question is: *what did I have to put in that email in order for you to be able to declare success?*

SUCCESS CHECKLIST FOR A SUCCESS CHECKLIST

Building a 'success checklist' is the quickest and most effective way to empower people to work towards a clear outcome/intent, instead of micromanaging them on the process. Here's my success checklist for making a success checklist:

1. Each success checklist refers to one specific project or task, and has a future date that represents the deadline for this success checklist to hold true.

2. Every bullet point passes the 'video camera test'. Each point describes an observable outcome: something concrete, and not a vague abstraction. For example, 'customers are satisfied' isn't observable and shouldn't be on the list; 'customers are raving about our product on social media' is.

3. Every bullet point is truly important for success. This means that you should boil things down to the top 5–10 requirements and focus on those, instead of giving a laundry list of wants.

4. You include any process requirements as well as outcome requirements ('The marketing assets are approved by the management board at least three weeks before the campaign start date').

5. You include any negative conditions as well as positive conditions. ('We've spent less than $50,000 on the project' or 'You didn't bother the IT team about this outside of the scheduled project meetings.')

The success checklist requires you to get specific. To complement this it's also a great idea to write a couple of sentences about the desired outcome and the broader contribution you want this project to make.

For example, 'This marketing campaign should reposition us in the eyes of our customers as a forward-looking and environmentally aware company. It should be the first thing that comes to mind whenever customers think of us, and it should get them excited about our other products and services. Ultimately we should be able to look back in three years and identify $50 million of sales that resulted directly or indirectly from this campaign.'

You can see that this broader vision is less specific and doesn't have a firm deadline, but it does provide very important context and 'feel'. Combine this 'vivid vision' with a specific 'success checklist' and you have a powerful tool for getting people aligned on any project you want to delegate.

Create your vivid vision and success checklist for one project that you want to delegate.

> *For a helpful template for delegating tasks, including a template for success checklists, head over to the book bonuses available at https://xquadrant.com/bookbonuses/*

CHAPTER 29

Tactics were never going to be enough

In this part, 'The Influence Challenge', we found that you cannot create more Strategic Time in a vacuum.

This is why so many people fail to make a real shift in their use of time. Tactics aren't enough, and jumping straight into implementation without winning the hearts and minds of your key stakeholders will result in failure. Your superiors, your peers and your reports all have their expectations, needs and wants. You need to influence them and have some bold conversations if you are to make a sustainable shift in how you operate within your organisation.

So, you've looked at how to create explicit agreements with your stakeholders that gives you both clarity on what can be expected. You've mapped out your high-value conversations according to the four-part structure of context, proposal, questions and agreement.

You've seen how any business is a complex system that will very easily settle into its lowest-energy configuration. You've identified the areas where you have become the 'adjustment factor' in the broader organisation, where your lack of boundaries is costing you dearly. And you've started to raise energy barriers to help the system around you unlearn the unhelpful habits and readjust to new and more appropriate ways of behaving.

Specifically, you've learned how to use the SCARS approach to make your team come to you with fully formed requests. And you've mastered the use of the Tentative button and the TRADE approach to raise energy barriers around accepting meeting requests from other people.

Finally, you've improved your delegation game and have seen how a visual 'success checklist' is the quickest and most effective way to empower people to work towards a clear outcome and intent, instead of micromanaging them on the process.

At this point, you might be feeling uncomfortable. You know the theory, but perhaps you're not putting it into practice. You're not sure there's really anything more you can do to free yourself up. In fact, you're wondering if it's actually possible, necessary or desirable.

If that's you, then turn the page to Part 4, *'The Mindset Challenge'*, where we'll get to the root cause of your overload. We'll play with your thinking, and we'll uncover the unconscious assumptions that are keeping you on the hamster wheel and away from all the benefits of Strategic Time.

Alternatively, you can choose your own adventure by heading back to page 28 and decide what your next priority area needs to be, or head over to the online assessment at **https://xquadrant.com/bookbonuses** for a personalised recommendation.

Part 4

THE MINDSET CHALLENGE

CHAPTER 30

It's all in your head, Mr Tweedy

The egg farm was about to be turned into a chicken pie business.

We're talking of course about the movie *Chicken Run*, the stop-motion animated adventure comedy film produced by DreamWorks Animation back in 2000.

The evil Mrs Tweedy, frustrated at the minuscule profits from her egg farm, decides to implement her chicken pie business plan, which is obviously very bad news for the chickens.

Her husband, Mr Tweedy, spots the chickens acting strangely and wonders if they are organised and plotting to escape, but Mrs Tweedy dismisses his beliefs: 'It's all in your head, Mr Tweedy!'

Two people, two views on reality, leading to two very different attitudes and behaviours.

In this part, we're going to think about the mindset challenge that you're facing. Because a shift in our thinking is necessary before we can really create a shift in our results.

We don't experience reality – we experience our *perception* of reality. To take a random example, we might have been passed over for a promotion – that's the raw fact – but what we experience is a *story* that our brain makes up about what that means.

We might tell ourselves that missing out on the promotion is a bad thing, that our boss is obviously playing favourites, that the person who won the promotion was using underhand tactics, that we never wanted to play office politics anyway. Or some other combination of thoughts. And so we feel upset, angry or whatever. The point is that our experience of the event is defined by the thoughts and meanings we attach to it, not the event itself. Perhaps missing that promotion is actually the best thing that could have happened to you!

Our perceptions, and the stories we tell ourselves, are actually the biggest barriers to freeing ourselves up for more strategic activity and to stepping up to a new level of impact. It's our mindset, our thoughts about what's *necessary*, what's *possible* and what's *desirable*, that are creating the world in which we think we live. And we respond accordingly.

> *It's our mindset, our thoughts about what's necessary, what's possible and what's desirable, that are creating the world in which we think we live. And we respond accordingly.*

IF YOU ARE BILL GATES, WHY ARE YOU TAKING OUT THE TRASH?

I worked with Kathy, the marketing director of a fast-growing IT infrastructure business. She told me, 'The problem is that I really don't have the time to work on the high-value activities I know I'm capable of. The senior leadership team continually pull me in to urgent lower-level issues. I've mentioned it to them, and they agree they should leave me to work on the big-picture stuff, but they don't actually change their behaviour.'

She felt stuck. If the founder of the company kept making these kinds of requests despite her attempts to push back… well, there was nothing she could do, right?

So I told her a story.

Imagine an entrepreneur manages to hire Bill Gates into his software start-up. He breathes a sigh of relief when he walks through the door.

'Bill! At last. Our rubbish bins are overflowing. Please take them out, will you?'

Bill obliges, and comes back a few minutes later ready to get coding. But then he's interrupted again. 'One more thing, Bill. We have an urgent parcel to deliver to a customer. It's just a couple of hours' drive. It's really important… could you just drop that off, please?'

Bill shrugs and takes the parcel, slightly surprised but accepting. The trip takes the rest of the day.

The next morning, as Bill is parking his car, the business owner runs up to him, bucket and sponge in hand. 'Morning, Bill. Before you start today, would you mind washing my car? I have a big meeting this afternoon and would like to turn up in a sparklingly clean vehicle.' And so Bill takes the bucket.

Let's pause there. If you'd hired Bill Gates to your software start-up, you'd be an absolute fool not to get him to work in his zone of genius, designing and coding incredible software. If you knew *who* you had hired, you wouldn't be giving him low-level tasks. It just wouldn't make sense.

So my challenge to Kathy was: how are you creating this situation where people are giving you the bucket and sponge, the lower-level tasks, when you know you could create ten times more value working in your zone of genius? What is it about how you are showing up that is making the founder believe that it's the rational decision for him offload these low-level tasks to you?

If you believe 'that's just the situation right now', there's nothing you can do. You may as well stop reading this book. You have no power to change anything.

But if you ask, 'how am I creating this reality?' then you have agency. You can show up as a leader and effect change.

In Kathy's case, she started by thinking that it wasn't possible to avoid the founder dumping tasks on her. However, as the Bill Gates anecdote reveals, there was another and more interesting option. She could turn up with such a compelling vision of the value she could contribute, and a plan to deliver that, that the founder would be crazy to distract her for anything else. A new and empowering possibility had emerged.

Kathy had been telling herself, 'That's just the way it is around here.' But in fact, her reality was something that she'd played a large part in creating.

DON'T BUY IN TO YOUR OWN STORIES

Let's put the spotlight on you now. What's necessary in *your* world? What are the things that are just imposed, the constraints that can't be changed? Perhaps it feels necessary to be available 24/7 on your work's instant messaging platform. Perhaps it feels necessary for you to follow up on all the customer support requests. Perhaps it feels necessary to deliver the board presentation every quarter. Well, what if they *weren't* actually necessary after all? What would that open up?

What's possible for you? Perhaps more importantly, what's impossible for you? Perhaps it feels impossible to have a certain conversation with your boss. Perhaps it feels impossible to say no to certain demands on your time. Perhaps it feels impossible to get your team to take more responsibility. But what if those things were possible after all? What would that open up?

What's desirable for you? Perhaps you feel it's important to deliver the best possible work, or to get back to your colleagues very promptly, or visit your top customers every month. Perhaps you feel it's desirable to make sure everyone in the team is comfortable... or uncomfortable. What if these things weren't actually desirable at all? What if the downsides actually outweighed the upsides? What would that open up?

As we go through this part, we'll look at some of the assumptions and thought patterns we bring to our work, and see whether we can reframe those to open up new possibilities for contribution and impact.

I often say to my clients, 'My job is to refuse to buy in to the stories you're telling yourself,' because these are the stories that confine us and limit us. When we change the story about what's necessary, what's possible and what's desirable, then everything shifts.

What are the stories you're telling yourself? What do you believe is necessary, possible and desirable for you right now? And if one of those beliefs wasn't actually true, which one would open up the most possibilities?

> You can find interactive tools to help you identify your top mindset roadblocks, along with the other resources for this book, at https://xquadrant.com/bookbonuses

CHAPTER 31

You're the High-Performing Janitor

'Why do you want to be the High-Performing Janitor?'

That woke him up.

Gareth was a finance executive in a multinational. He managed a small finance team and reported in to the country manager. And he was seriously overloaded! Several of the company's core finance processes, including sales commissions and payroll, depended on his direct involvement.

And whilst Gareth's team were competent, he didn't feel they had the knowledge or skills to deliver at the same level of quality and reliability as him.

As he put it, 'I'm not really able to delegate because I need to know the job is getting done to a high standard.'

The problem of course with this line of thinking is that by obsessing over your current set of tasks, you are failing to add value in more significant ways. And so I introduced him to what I call 'the High-Performing

Janitor syndrome'. It's a tongue-in-cheek image aimed at giving a new perspective on what's happening.

Why be the High-Performing Janitor, cleaning the floor to perfection, when you could be the high-performing executive, leading strategic initiatives that create new business opportunities or capabilities?

Are you going to be amazing at low-value tasks, or are you going to improve your ability to deliver the high-value tasks?

THERE'S NOTHING PERFECT ABOUT PERFECTIONISM

You know you're the High-Performing Janitor if you do everything in your job well. It's basically perfectionism rearing its head.

The problem with the word 'perfectionism', however, is that it has the word 'perfect' in it, and that sounds like a good thing. We might bemoan our perfectionist tendencies, but deep down we're quite proud of our high standards. There's nothing wrong with having high standards of course, but perfectionism is a fear-based strategy aimed at avoiding failure or harsh judgment, and it results in symptoms such as procrastination, a tendency to avoid challenges, rigid thinking, unhealthy comparisons, and a lack of creativity.

So embrace being the learner. Embrace being imperfect. If you're pretty darn good at everything you do, you're not leaning into challenge, learning and growth. You're stuck in your comfort zone. Perhaps it's time to raise your game. Stop being the High-Performing Janitor, polishing those floor tiles to perfection, and give yourself a mental promotion!

YOU'RE THE HIGH-PERFORMING JANITOR

If you're pretty darn good at everything you do, you're not leaning into challenge, learning and growth.

What keeps people in High-Performing Janitor mode? Often it's the fear of Imposter Syndrome. As a mentor of mine, Rich Litvin, likes to say, 'Imposter Syndrome is a feature, not a bug!' If you feel Imposter Syndrome, you are growing and stretching and making new things happen. It means you are breaking new ground, and it's helping you stay in a posture of learning instead of complacency. Putting it another way, Imposter Syndrome actually just means your inner confidence is lower than your external competence!

Here was another argument I gave Gareth, which might help if you're undecided. Being the High-Performing Janitor is unethical and unproductive. There were key operational processes that only he could perform. He'd unwittingly created a single point of failure in the organisation, which is incredibly risky. Delegation has to happen!

At the heart of High-Performing Janitor syndrome is a focus on present performance over future contribution. A preference for performance over learning. A desire for comfort, instead of getting comfortable with discomfort. And it kills your ability to step up to a new level of impact.

Where are you hanging on to the mop and bucket of the High-Performing Janitor? Where you are staying in the comfort zone?

CHAPTER 32

When trustworthy becomes untrustworthy

He thought the problem was his email workflow. But what he discovered would rock his world…

Julian had just been promoted to Chief Human Resources Officer of a global IT services firm operating in some twenty countries. New to the C-Suite, he'd asked me to support him in making the biggest possible impact as he stepped up to the new challenge, and we'd identified some major transformational projects that he was now championing.

'I'm finding it hard to give the strategic projects the focus they deserve,' he began our conversation one day. 'There are so many pulls on my time, and I seem to spend hours on end responding to emails. I need some email management tips.'

When clients start by asking me for 'tips', a mental alarm sounds. It's almost never what they really need. Anyone can Google productivity tips, but what most leaders need is a shift in their thinking and a fresh perspective. So we started exploring: what exactly was the problem?

'Well, I like to keep my inbox under control,' he explained. 'I don't want to be a bottleneck, stopping other people from getting on with their jobs, and I don't want to be the kind of person who you have to remind three times before getting an answer. I'm a team player. I want to be trustworthy and reliable. But right now I'm drowning in emails.'

'At this point,' I explained, 'there's no tip or trick I can give you that will get you out of your inbox.' Seeing his look of surprise, I continued. 'Your behaviour is a natural extension of your values, right? You're a team player. You want to be trustworthy, reliable. So you turn around emails fast and keep a clean inbox. If I tell you to be less trustworthy, less reliable, and less of a team player you're not going to be interested. Am I right?'

He nodded his agreement.

'But let me ask you something,' I continued. 'If your CEO was here right now, what would he want you to be focusing on?'

'Oh, the big transformational projects,' he replied. 'He's really excited about those and can see the value.'

'Perfect. How about the investors,' I continued, 'what would they be asking?'

'Same thing. These projects will free up our workforce for more productive activities.'

'And the employees themselves, what would they be asking if they were in this room with us?'

'Hmmm. I guess they'd want me to work on the strategic projects too. They're fed up of the archaic systems we use and are desperate for a simpler and more modern employee experience.'

I continued to probe. 'And the customers?'

'Well... It doesn't affect them directly, but I suppose, yes, once we have these projects implemented our people will be freed up to spend less time on internal admin and more time serving clients. So they'd want me to deliver the big projects too.'

It was time to turn the heat up.

'What I'm hearing is this,' I summarised. 'Your CEO, your investors, your employees, your customers – they all want you to be focused on delivering these transformational initiatives. Putting it another way, these projects are actually why you're getting paid the big bucks! So, let me put it to you: when you are stuck in your inbox, processing low-level requests, you're not being a trustworthy and reliable team player. You're being an untrustworthy and unreliable Chief Human Resources Officer.'

It was an insight moment. His identity shifted. He didn't need an email management tip from me. He had what he needed.

SERVE STAKEHOLDERS, DON'T PLEASE PEOPLE

Stop people-pleasing. It's a defence mechanism to make you feel good in the short term and to keep you out of awkward conversations.

But pleasing people is NOT serving your stakeholders.

Pleasing people generally means you're responding to whoever is shouting the loudest. As I've said before, every 'yes' to one person is a 'no' to someone else. So start thinking about who's not in the room. What are the more significant needs that you're saying 'no' to right now because you're saying 'yes' to the noise?

> *What are the more significant needs that you're saying 'no' to right now because you're saying 'yes' to the noise?*

Pleasing people means you're giving them what they want, not necessarily what they need. So what's the highest value you can actually bring right now? What's the greatest and most valuable service you can undertake?

Like Julian, if you try to please people you will find you actually undermine your impact. You'll stop delivering your highest contribution. And the trap is, you'll still feel productive and useful.

So, commit to serving your stakeholders, instead of pleasing the people who are shouting the loudest.

Commit to working on the things that will create a real impact. Commit to giving those things the attention and focus they need. Commit to being trustworthy and reliable, by using your 'time, talents and treasure' in the most impactful way possible.

Put contribution ahead of popularity.

In what contexts do you need to shift from pleasing people to serving stakeholders?

CHAPTER 33

You say responsive. I say distracted

'It's really important for me to be responsive,' David explained. 'I want to be the high performer who gets back to people quickly.'

The problem was that David's responsiveness was holding him back from a greater level of contribution.

You say responsive. I say distracted.

In our always-on, always-connected culture, it's easy for responsiveness to become over-responsiveness. In fact, we often take pride in the speed at which we deal with incoming requests. But over-responsiveness creates a whole raft of problems.

The first problem with over-responsiveness is that you train people to rely on your instantaneous responses. The more responsive you are, the more people will rely on you. But whilst this sounds good and it often feels good, they're actually relying on you for the wrong things, for the lower-level activity that is keeping you away from your next level of impact.

The second problem with over-responsiveness is that you give people the easy option. If it's easier and quicker to ask you than to do their own research, remember who they should be calling about this, or build their own skill set, then the chances are they'll keep taking that shortcut and reaching out to you.

You also increase the communications flow and end up with more on your plate. Email begets email. You open the gates of infinity a little bit wider, and more pours in.

The fourth issue is that you spend time on problems that would have resolved themselves anyway. Have you ever returned from vacation and started to clean up your email, to find that most of the threads in your inbox have pretty much resolved themselves in your absence, allowing you to confidently hit the 'delete' key?

Most importantly, over-responsiveness pulls you away from your high-value activities and your most important Improvement Project, and into the easy buzz of lower-level work. It ensnares you deeper into the Infinity Trap, and it undermines your overall impact.

YOU'RE IMPORTANT, TOO

You're thinking, 'But I'm a high performer. I need to be responsive.'

Imagine you needed to contact someone important. Your CEO or the Chairman of the Board. The president or the prime minister. The head of a Fortune 100 company. Would you expect them to be hyper-responsive to your message?

No. You understand they have many responsibilities and projects, and they aren't going to drop everything when an email from you comes in.

The world's greatest leaders know the dangers of over-responsiveness. As a general, Napoleon enforced a delay in responding to letters, ordering his secretary to wait a full three weeks before opening any correspondence. Just like when we clean up our email after a vacation, he found that most of the letters no longer needed his attention.

You need to create a barrier between you and the constant inflow of requests. And, as Ryan Holiday puts it in his book *Stillness Is the Key*:

> 'The first thing great chiefs of staff do [...] is limit the amount of people who have access to the boss. They become gatekeepers: no more drop-ins, tidbits, and stray reports. So the boss can see the big picture. So the boss has time and room to think. Because if the boss doesn't? Well, then nobody can.'

Let's put the focus back on you. Who are you, anyway? You might not be president or prime minister, but you're an accomplished and skilled individual, with some key transformational projects to deliver. You, too, have many pulls on your time that threaten to distract you. You are an important person as well. And important people aren't over-responsive. They don't do knee-jerk reactions. They are considered. They are strategic. And they don't let themselves be sucked into trivia.

Over-responsiveness is a form of people-pleasing. Once again, we're jumping when people say 'jump', and we're failing to spot the more important things we're saying 'no' to.

Moreover, over-responsiveness is linked to us holding on to habits that no longer serve us. When we start our careers, success often comes from saying yes to everything and turning requests around as quickly as possible. But as we take on more responsibility and start working on more impactful projects, this 'success habit' of hyper-responsiveness starts to work against us. Hyper-responsiveness traps us in operations, keeps us working on other people's problems, and distracts us from the real value we are there to provide.

Until you acknowledge that you are important and your time is important, and realise that you don't need to respond immediately when requests come in, you'll remain scattered and distracted and won't live up your potential.

> *Hyper-responsiveness traps us in operations, keeps us working on other people's problems, and distracts us from the real value we are there to provide.*

When I raised this with David, a participant in one of our public *Impact Accelerator* programmes, the penny dropped. He was a senior manager with some important projects to deliver. He didn't need to be at the beck and call of the whole organisation. He didn't need to provide a knee-jerk response to every issue that came his way.

So, commit to leaving behind over-responsiveness and become considered and strategic instead. Start to see yourself as the important leader you are. Your time is precious and it doesn't serve the greater good to have it scattered across a thousand minor requests. Many leaders have an open-door policy, but this simply means you can be interrupted at any time. By all means, have certain times when you're available to your team, but make sure there are times when you have a closed-door policy too.

It's time to be considered instead of knee-jerk.

Where is over-responsiveness showing up in your life and work? And what are the beliefs that are causing this pattern to continue?

CHAPTER 34

What if the problem with your team... was you?

Now let's think about your team.

Actually, let's think about your *thinking* about your team.

As I've said, our mindset reflects what we currently believe is necessary, possible and desirable. So it's important to think about what we believe is necessary, possible and desirable when it comes to our team.

What are your current beliefs regarding your team and your ability to delegate the lower-level activity to them? In other words, why haven't you delegated the operational activity to them already?

Perhaps you'll say:

They don't have the skills.

They're already overloaded.

They're not committed enough.

They don't have the experience.

They don't understand the politics.

Every time we start thinking like this, we need to catch ourselves. As a leader, your job isn't to manage tasks. It's to manage people. So it's time to revisit your limiting beliefs about your people.

> **As a leader, your job isn't to manage tasks. It's to manage people.**

They don't have the skills or the experience. And neither did you, once. Many leaders had to figure things out the hard way, by experience and with minimal input, and yet they procrastinate on delegating those same tasks because they haven't been able to find the time to write an end-to-end instruction manual for their team! How can you support your team in the building of the necessary skills, instead of telling them exactly what to do at every stage in the process?

They're already overloaded. Yes, for two reasons. Firstly, because we live in the world of infinity – so it's the default pattern for everyone unless we get strategic and intentional. Secondly, because if you are modelling a life of overload and crazy-busy, this is the culture you will create in your team. Perhaps they need some inspiring high-value activities to do, so they start to think about how they can clear the decks. Perhaps you need to take them through the CRASH approach.

They're not committed enough. What if commitment is an output, not an input? What if you, as their leader, have *not yet created the conditions in which commitment naturally arises*? Have you really given them a vision for why what they do is important? Have you given them a sense of responsibility and autonomy? Are you overriding their decisions, solving their problems, protecting them from the consequences of underperformance? *Think less about their commitment level and more about your leadership level.*

> **Think less about your team's commitment level and more about your leadership level.**

They don't understand the politics. The organisational context and the politics at play can be complex, but this isn't an insurmountable obstacle. Tell your team about the issues. Take them with you to meetings. Or just trust them to figure it out as they go.

The truth is your team are able to do much more than you think. We systematically underestimate other people.

After going through our *Impact Accelerator* public programme, one client, Ali, found that her team was able to take on far more than she ever imagined. She told me, 'I cannot do it all, and I am not expected to do it all. The biggest mindset shift was accepting that as a higher-up manager I am no longer the person who should be the 'worker bee'. I need to be in a comfortable place where my mind and time are freed up to address higher-level problems, review, and approve items.

'I have to keep resisting the urge to do everything myself! Before I dig in and do the work myself I stop and question "who else should be doing this?" since the answer cannot be "me" all the time. It's taken a very conscious effort, but I've made tremendous progress with that shift.'

YOU HAVE CREATED THE TEAM YOU DESERVE

Some teams are ambitious, daring, caring. Others are lethargic, boring and cold. And it could be the same people in both teams! What's the difference? Team culture.

The truth is, the culture within your team makes a huge difference to how your people show up. And you, as leader, shape that culture. In other words, you're responsible for the dynamics that you're seeing in your team.

> *You're responsible for the dynamics that you're seeing in your team.*

Team culture is influenced by the levels of support and challenge that you, the leader, provide over time.

Providing CHALLENGE means setting ambitious goals, maintaining accountability, providing candid feedback on current performance, challenging people to go beyond what they feel they can currently achieve, and instilling a productive tension into the relationship.

Giving SUPPORT means building a relationship that goes beyond getting things done, encouraging and motivating the team, investing time and energy in growing people's skills and confidence, and creating security and trust in the relationship.

When we consistently bring both high support and high challenge to our team, we create what I call an 'ACTIVATOR' style of leadership where people know we are 'for them' and that we aren't going to let them stag-

LEADERSHIP MATRIX

HIGH SUPPORT

INSULATOR — Stagnation & dependency	**ACTIVATOR** — Growth & commitment
ABDICATOR — Apathy & inertia	**DOMINATOR** — Survival & compliance

LOW CHALLENGE ← → **HIGH CHALLENGE**

LOW SUPPORT

nate but push them to become the best they can be. We bring high levels of challenge, but also the requisite level of care and support.

Activators create a real sense of trust, empowerment, ownership and opportunity and represent the 'gold standard' of leadership. It doesn't mean you're 'jamming on the accelerator and the brakes at the same time', but it does mean you're constantly deciding who needs more support, and who needs more challenge, to give the entire team what they need.

The issue is that no one is a natural-born Activator. It's always a learned leadership behaviour. Instead, our natural tendency will be to gravitate to one of the other quadrants. Perhaps we're naturally strong at support, or at challenge, or perhaps we're more introverted and find it easy to withdraw from the team. So when we're accidental in our leadership, or when we're under pressure, we're highly likely to find ourselves in a different quadrant:

The DOMINATOR leader brings high challenge but fails to bring the same level of support, so the team feels fearful, stressed and like 'pawns on the chessboard'. They'll likely comply with your instructions out of survival instinct, but will become increasingly demotivated and cynical.

If you have tendencies to operate in this quadrant, you'll find yourself in a vicious circle, where you end up increasing the pressure and making the decisions, which reduces the level of ownership in the team – to which you respond by increasing the pressure and making even more decisions.

The INSULATOR leader creates a warm team environment, bringing high levels of support, but fails to have the hard conversations about performance and behaviour standards with the team. This creates a 'comfort zone' that's pleasant on one level but actually results in dependency and stagnation for the team.

If you're operating in this quadrant, you're not bringing enough accountability and productive tension to your team, and you are tolerating low standards. Typically, the team wraps up relatively early, whilst you end up working late to compensate for deliverables that are not up to scratch, and you start to believe the team are incapable of greater things.

The ABDICATOR leader actually withdraws from the team, perhaps so the leader can 'figure things out' by themselves or perhaps due to their own sense of fatigue or disinterest. The team becomes bored, with little motivation to do anything but the minimum, with a culture of apathy and inertia.

Pause for a second and apply this model to yourself. Where would your team place you on this framework? What might you need to adjust to be more consistently operating from the Activator position? Who needs more challenge from you, and who needs more support?

DECIDE TO TRUST YOUR TEAM

At the heart of all this is a question of trust. Do you trust your team?

Make it a decision. Will you choose to trust your team? And what needs to happen for that to become a reality?

Give them big challenges. Develop them. Believe in them. Be there for them when they need it, but not when they don't.

Stop thinking 'can I delegate more?' and start thinking '*how* can I delegate more?'

What leadership culture are you creating in your team, and how can you better create an Activator culture? Does your team need more challenge from you right now? Or do they need more support?

CHAPTER 35

You are productive... too productive

'You can't shift gear when your foot is jammed on the accelerator.'

Action. Progress. Results.

So many of us build our success with that formula. And it works when we're at a junior level. We're driven, determined and we love moving fast. Guilty as charged!

The issue is that there's a visceral pull towards the adrenaline and the action. We can feel guilty when we're not in production mode, when we're not driving things forward, when we're not in the whirlwind.

So many leaders are restless, driven and determined to maximise results. That's why the Infinity Trap is such a snare. We find out that we're good at solving problems and can operate at higher speeds than many of our colleagues, and that underpins our success in the first part of our career. We relentlessly continue in that vein, pushing, driving and controlling. It's incredibly tiring but it's the only way we know to really deliver results.

I put it to you that your next level of success will come from less action and more reflection.

In his book *Hell Yeah or No*, founder of CD Baby Derek Sivers describes how he used to complete a forty-three-minute cycle ride a few times each week along the beach in Santa Monica, California. He'd be full-on, red-faced sprinting, and exhausted by the end. After a few months, he decided to take it easy. Dial down the effort to just 50 per cent. Enjoy the ride, take in the view as he went. When he finished this incredibly enjoyable circuit, he found he'd completed it in forty-five minutes. The extra effort he normally put in – that additional 50 per cent – gave him only a 4 per cent boost. And what a difference in experience! He concludes, 'When I notice that I'm driving myself to exhaustion, I remember that bike ride and try dialling back my effort by 50 percent. It's been amazing how often everything gets done just as well and just as fast, with what feels like half the effort.'

> *Your next level of success will come from less action and more reflection.*

If you ever take a lesson to drive a sports car around a racetrack, you'll likely to be told, 'Go slow to go smooth, and go smooth to go fast.' This is a lesson I need to learn anew every day, so great is my bias for getting things done. I have a pewter snail on my desk as a physical and permanent reminder to *slow down to speed up*. It's not just a cute phrase; it's a strategic imperative, because when we create time away from operational distractions and slow down our thinking, breakthroughs occur.

In his book *Stillness Is the Key*, author Ryan Holiday recounts the story of how President John F. Kennedy defused the Cuban missile crisis. His advisors were emphatic: attack swiftly to destroy the Cuban missile sites. Kennedy pushed back, took his time to think through the consequences that would inevitably follow, adopted a different strategy (a blockade), and generally slowed things down in order to give Khrushchev time to reconsider and find an acceptable, peaceful way to resolve the situation.

To quote Holiday:

> 'This is, in fact, the first obligation of a leader and a decision maker. Our job is not to "go with our gut" or fixate on the first impression we form about an issue [...] Because if the leader can't take the time to develop a clear sense of the bigger picture, who will? If the leader isn't thinking through all the way to the end, who is?'

What he's getting at is the need to think several layers deep. Whilst the first-order implications of a decision are often simple to see, the second-order and third-order ripple effects are often much more significant and can be counterintuitive. Whilst some courses of action immediately present themselves, thinking more carefully might reveal exponentially better approaches. Thinking matters, and good thinking requires time.

Thinking can make us feel lazy and even induce guilt. 'My team are so busy, can I really justify going for a walk by the lake?' Yes!

Remember the Infinity Trap? The pull towards massive action and hyper productivity is real, but when action and productivity crowd out reflection your leadership impact takes a downward trajectory.

You see, in any moment, you have a choice. You can be productive, or you can be creative. You can apply brute force, or you can use your brain. Thoughtfulness and creativity have far greater leverage.

In any moment, you have a choice. You can be productive, or you can be creative.

So I'll say it: you are probably too productive!

Our problem is often that thinking is ambiguous, difficult and unrewarding… until we get the breakthrough. We're so accustomed to the adrenaline rush of being in the thick of the action that entering into quiet reflection can feel unnatural and unproductive. The act of slowing down to think isn't going to get recognition or reward. It's the unglamorous deep work at the heart of any strategic leader. But from that place of reflection will come the insights, the breakthroughs and the shifts that will create your next level of success.

How much time do you actually spend thinking and being creative?

CHAPTER 36

You're addicted to firefighting

Most leaders know the Eisenhower Matrix, the distinction between urgent tasks and important tasks. And most people feel they are doing a good job if they spend most of their time addressing the top priority tasks – those that are both urgent and important.

But there's another name for urgent/important tasks: firefighting. 'I got pulled into some firefighting all of last week,' we say – but it's a humble-brag. It's a complaint, but we quite like the connotations: firefighters are heroes, right? There's a sense of sacrifice and bravery inherent in the term 'firefighting'.

But in the real world, if you're firefighting then your house is literally burning to the ground, your family are in peril, there are toxic fumes everywhere, your furniture is ruined, and your carefully planned vacation and tomorrow's theatre excursion are definitely off. Firefighting is a *terrible* situation to be in.

If you secretly love firefighting then you're creating a self-perpetuating cycle. Your colleagues will often find it easier to call the fire brigade than to build the systems and processes that would prevent the fire in the first place. In business, fighting fires actually takes the pressure off the real root cause issues being addressed. Firefighting is mainly the consequence of bad systems and processes.

From time to time, of course, jumping in to solve important and urgent problems is necessary, and is part of being part of a larger team. Nobody expects the unexpected! But we must be on our guard not to take firefighting on as a heroic identity. Helping a colleague, customer or partner out now and again is fine, but repeatedly coming to their aid is actually enabling and perpetuating systems and processes that aren't working properly. We're back into the world of people-pleasing instead of impact and contribution.

In the Eisenhower Matrix, then, the urgent/important zone (i.e. firefighting) should actually be described as 'the nasty surprises and broken business processes zone'.

So every time you find yourself firefighting, stuck in the hamster wheel of the urgent and important, ask yourself what the fix needs to be to stop the fire recurring. Be a fire prevention officer, not a firefighter. Get yourself into the important, non-urgent zone, which is where you'll find your top improvement projects and your meaningful strategic work.

Be a fire prevention officer, not a firefighter.

As a leader, you can make this happen. Why not adopt the '72 hour rule' that some businesses use, which goes like this:

If we need to ask a colleague to unexpectedly turn something around in less than seventy-two hours, it's a sign of a broken business process and we need to fix it.

Imagine the difference in your working environment, in your productivity, and in your ability to deliver real progress if the root causes behind all urgent requests in your organisation were gradually and systematically addressed. That's a game-changer.

How can you be less of a firefighter and more of a fire prevention officer?

CHAPTER 37

Make contribution your North Star

It all comes down to one thing, really.

Our mindset issues, whether it's perfectionism, people-pleasing, over-responsiveness, not trusting our team, being overly restless and driven to overachieve, or your own particular brand of hangup, come down to fear.

Fear of what people will think.

Fear of being 'found out'.

Fear of failure.

You see, it's not your boss, your team, your company culture or your productivity habits that are keeping you from your next level of impact. It's fear.

Haley is an incredibly impressive leader. She's risen to the top of her (very male-dominated) organisation. She's created incredible loyalty in her team, and her span of control has multiplied in recent years. In her personal life, she's climbed to Base Camp on Mount Everest. She's scaled Kilimanjaro. She's taken on triathlons, marathons, you name it.

Despite her external success, she was still held back by fear. Fear of applying for a 'bigger role'. Fear of external visibility and public speaking. She was the organisation's best-kept secret!

For her, it was about fear of incompetence; of being an imposter; of failing.

As we worked on this, a couple of key distinctions really helped.

Firstly, fear is just a word. It's describing a physiological and mental state, or some thoughts we are having, but we can label that experience as we prefer. Is it fear, or it is excitement? An adrenaline rush? The feeling you get when you tackle a challenging black ski slope? Perhaps it's not a thing to run away from; perhaps it's your internal GPS showing you which way to head.

For millennia, our fear response was a way of keeping us safe from imminent physical danger. In our current professional context, however, our fear response is being triggered by imaginary threats – a long chain of invented what-ifs that, if you follow the rabbit hole, take you mentally from flubbing an important presentation to being destitute on the streets unable to provide for your family.

Secondly, confidence is a result and not a requirement. Does a baby wait for confidence before taking her first step? Does a learner driver slip into the drivers' seat for the first time full of confidence? No, confidence comes when we look in the rear-view mirror and see what we've already accomplished. What you need instead is commitment to your goal and courage to act.

Thirdly, safe is dangerous; dangerous is safe. We confuse safety with predictability, and we confuse danger with volatility. But oftentimes what looks like safety is actually the path of stagnation and a gradual loss of capability. Think of the person in a 'safe' but boring corporate job, taking home their monthly pay cheque until one day they are laid off and they find their skills are outdated, their contacts stale, and their salary expectations unjustifiable.

What looks like the risky path often turns out to be much safer.

By the same token, what looks like the risky path often turns out to be much safer. As Nassim Nicholas Taleb writes in his excellent book *Antifragile*, think of the person who builds a freelance business. Their income is much more volatile than a salaried employee, but they become highly attuned to the needs of the market, they diversify their revenue streams across many clients, and they keep their skills current. This means they can face the future much more confidently than most employees, who have all their eggs in the basket of their current employer.

Generally, whatever causes us to learn and grow is the safe path; whatever keeps us busy but comfortable is the dangerous path.

FEAR VS. CONTRIBUTION

Instead of giving in to fear, choose courage and contribution.

Fear is a prison created by an excessive sense of self-preservation. Contribution is the way to break out of that prison. When we commit to a cause, a purpose, an act of service, then we get out of our own way and we become unstoppable. It's no longer about us, it's about the impact we're making on others.

Imagine you were to give a speech in front of a stadium full of spectators. Fifty thousand people. For many of us, this would be a scary experience. We're thinking about ourselves, and we're getting fearful.

Now let's imagine there are lives at stake. If everyone in the stadium donated five dollars you could save 10,000 children from imminent death. Suddenly, you have a purpose. Whilst the adrenaline will be pumping, the chances of you walking onto that stage are hugely increased, and your ability to deliver a passionate and compelling message has skyrocketed.

The difference between the two scenarios? Your sense of contribution.

The attractiveness of the Infinity Trap is it gives us an excuse to hide behind our busyness. It's an easy excuse for staying in our comfort zone and not taking the courageous steps to break through our wall of fear, whatever it may be for us.

Catrin, a client, expressed this insight really nicely, saying, 'Believing that I'm so crazy-busy is actually a protective mechanism, because it means no one can ask any more of me.'

But today, I'm calling you to turn in the direction of your fear, and face it. But instead of trying to overcome it, look beyond it to the impact and contribution you can truly make. What's the highest way you can serve, the greatest value you can bring?

Commit to contributing at your highest level.

CHAPTER 38

Be Superman. Or Batman

I had some troubles naming this chapter.

I originally called it 'Be Superman, Not Batman'. Both accomplish extraordinary things. But whilst Batman relies on a whole set of external tools and gadgets to create his 'superhero effect', Superman harnesses his authentic natural powers.

It felt like Batman relied on external factors, and Superman was the real deal. Many leaders rely on tools, tips and techniques to control or manipulate people, and plough through their to-do list. But the best leaders bring an inner strength and commitment that's the real secret of their success.

However, I then realised I could also call this chapter 'Be Batman, Not Superman'.

Superman spends most of his time as Clark Kent. He steps aside from his power to blend in, and comes across as mild, inoffensive and ineffective. He's dialled down his impact.

On the other hand, Bruce Wayne creates himself as Batman. He made the decision to step up to a new level of impact. Sure, there were some tools and gadgets to help. But what makes Batman a hero isn't the tool belt, but his character: the commitment, courage, determination, and sense of justice that he embodies. It was the quality of Bruce Wayne's thinking and the force of his character that made him powerful.

Both embody the path. Pick whichever one you want. But the truth is this: your to-be list is more powerful than your to-do list. Who you are becoming is more important than what you are doing.

> *Your to-be list is more powerful than your to-do list. Who you are becoming is more important than what you are doing.*

You, my friend, are Clark Kent. Are you going to stop hiding and embody your full potential as Superman? The phone box is right over there.

And you are also Bruce Wayne. Are you going to create a more powerful and impactful version of yourself, to make the contribution that you know is possible?

WHAT'S YOUR TO-BE LIST?

As a mentor of mine likes to say, 'You don't get what you want; you get who you are.' So deeper change is going to come through this question of who you want to be.

Imagine you're in sales. What's your to-do list for the day? Perhaps it's to make ten sales calls, send some proposals, follow up with some clients, and so forth. But what's your *to-be* list? What are the attitudes that will make it so much easier to accomplish all your tasks and goals over time?

> 'You don't get what you want;
> you get who you are.'

Well, if you come to work enthusiastic, curious, rested, attentive and with a desire to serve your clients' long-term good, you're vastly more likely to create a sustainable and successful business than if you come to work cynical, tired, bored and with a transactional, short-term mindset. Who you are *being* will have a material impact on your sales results!

As you think about freeing yourself up for more strategic and impactful activity, here are two words to be thinking about.

Firstly, courage. One thing all heroes possess is a preference for contribution over fear. It's hard to be a hero without courage. If you want to create a new level of impact, you are going to need to make some bold decisions. Have some courageous conversations. Experiment with new ideas. Lead at a new level.

Secondly, commitment. It's hard to be courageous without being committed to something greater than yourself. What is it that you are totally committed to?

Committed and courageous are two great candidates for your to-be list.

What's on your to-be list?

CHAPTER 39

WWXD

WWXD is a simple tool for thinking about your high-value activities AND your to-be list.

Some Christians put the letters 'WWJD' on bracelets or other visible articles, and it reminds them to ask themselves 'what would Jesus do?' when facing any kind of challenging situation or difficult decision in their daily lives. It's a quick way of getting outside their own thinking. Instead of consulting a priest, or finding time to study the Bible, they can ask themselves: well, what would Jesus do? And they'll find a new answer, perhaps a more loving and generous answer, than their instinctive response. As a Christian myself, I've found this question helpful at times, but no matter your religious or philosophical convictions this same approach can be broadened out and used on a wider variety of business questions.

MEET 'SUPER LEADER'

Imagine that, for some reason, you left your current leadership role. And two years later you meet a former colleague, and they tell you about your successor. They nailed it! They created amazing progress: they achieved all the goals you'd been talking about, they'd been promoted, they were making a huge difference. They'd really had an amazing twenty-four months.

Now tell me: what was that person doing? How did they achieve success? What kind of person were they? What were their habits? What did they do differently from you?

Don't describe background characteristics ('they had a lot more experience and many more contacts than me'). Instead describe their behaviours and their attitudes.

For example, their behaviours might be 'they spent a lot more time getting alignment with the CEO, and they were always making calls to see customers'. Even more important are their attitudes and way of *being*: 'they were always incredibly positive and energetic'.

Grab a notepad right now. Go ahead and write down a few bullets on each aspect. What are their key behaviours and what are their key attitudes and ways of being?

You now have an incredible roadmap for success. You now know how 'super leader' – the person known as X – created such impact, so why not be that person yourself?

In the future, when you're facing a decision, ask yourself WWXD ('What would X do?') to reconnect with this highly successful individual and find a bolder, more courageous way forward.

What would 'super leader' do, if they had your job?

A worksheet for this exercise can be accessed as part of the book bonuses at https://xquadrant.com/bookbonuses/

CHAPTER 40

Keep it front of mind

It's easy to think about mindset. It's another thing to choose a different path. We need some tools to help us make the shift. This story might help. In full disclosure, I've forgotten the precise details, but the overall thrust of the story is accurate.

There was a dinner party hosted by a famous businessmen and he invited a bunch of the great and the good to a high-end restaurant. The conversation was lively, the drinks were being served, and the host made an announcement. 'Before we go any further,' he began, 'I just want to say there's only one rule tonight: don't be negative. Any negativity, any bitching, any complaining about people means you need to put $50 in the pot in the middle of the table. Let's just keep it positive. Everyone OK with that?'

The other guests concurred. They were all successful, optimistic, future-focused people and so they all agreed that negativity wasn't helpful and it'd be easy for them to comply.

Within about ten minutes, there were hundreds and hundreds of dollars in the middle of the table! Everybody contributed multiple times, apart from one person.

Remember, these were intelligent, successful people that had just been told very clearly what was expected; there was an immediate consequence for breaking the rule; and there was immediate visual feedback every time people spoke negatively about others and had to put money into the pot. But despite the cards being stacked in their favour in all these ways, everybody kept breaking the rule. The wine was flowing, and so was the banter – and a bit of cynicism and complaint kept seeping into the conversation.

So they turned to the one person who hadn't put broken the rule and asked, 'How are you doing it? How are you the only one of us who hasn't had to put money into the pot?'

He smiled. 'It's simple, really. When you said what the rule was I picked up my place card.' He lifted up the small folded piece of cardboard that had his name on one side. 'And I turned it around, and I just wrote on the back of it: "NO NEGATIVITY!" Then I put it down in front of my wine glass. And so every time I picked up my wine, I saw it. I had this constant visual reminder of who I wanted to be in this moment.'

We don't think we need such tricks and techniques. They feel too basic, too much like a crutch. They feel like tips for beginners, and surely we should be past that kind of thing by now? But no, we always need a reminder to get off our tram lines and out of our default settings, and choose a different way of being.

Let's be the person with the place card, and not the person putting $50 into the 'oops, I did it again' jar. Take your to-be list and stick it to your computer screen, write it on your whiteboard, or set a recurring reminder on your phone. Whatever it takes for it to be a constant reminder to you.

SET YOUR VOLUME AND TONE

Electric guitars and amplifiers have volume and tone dials, and they need to be set consciously if an artist is to have the desired effect. Very often at the start of a meeting I'll say to the attendees, 'Let's pause for thirty seconds. Who do you want to be in this moment? Take a second to set your metaphorical volume and tone dials.'

To set your volume, write down a number from one to ten that reflects your typical volume level in the particular setting in which you find yourself. Some of us are loud and extraverted, and we may find our typical volume is an eight or more. Others are quieter and may struggle to be heard in meetings, with a volume of four or less. Once you have that number, set an intention for your desired volume level for the present meeting. Perhaps you'll choose to dial it down a bit, or dial it up a bit. Either way, you've made an intentional choice.

To set your tone, simply write down three adjectives that describe how you want to show up in this meeting. You might decide to show up as 'bold, uncompromising, direct' or 'curious, interested, friendly' or 'collaborative, principled, warm'. The act of writing these words down allows you to thoughtfully determine what needs to be on your to-be list in this moment.

Setting your volume and tone as you begin each day or enter a specific meeting helps you to pause and become mindful. It's a way of stopping for just a few seconds to remember what's on your 'place card' and reconnect to your to-be list.

VOLUME AND TONE

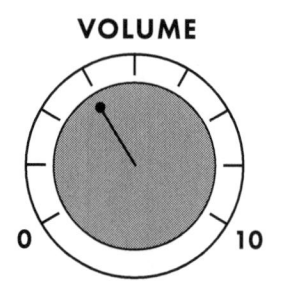

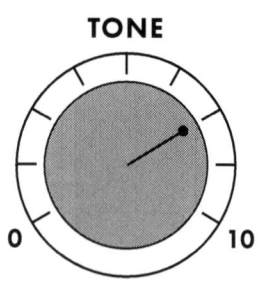

VOLUME 0–10

TONE 0–10

If you're serious about being the person who operates at a more strategic level, setting your volume and tone is an incredibly practical and effective way of turning all of this discussion on mindset into actionable steps to create a concrete reality.

Put your to-be list somewhere you're going to see it.

Your to-be list needs to be deployed. Put it somewhere visible where it will act as a constant reminder of your desired behaviours.

CHAPTER 41

On dragons and demons

Every hero starts their journey intending to slay the dragon, the monster that's creating death and destruction all around. But there comes a point where the protagonist realises that it's his or her inner fears – their demons – that are the biggest challenge to be overcome. Luke Skywalker had to master his anger before the Emperor could be dealt with. Frodo had to give up any hope of returning to the Shire before the One Ring could be destroyed in Mount Doom.

There's no slaying the dragon before the inner demons are dealt with.

Most leaders believe they have no choice but to be crazy-busy, given all the pressures and demands on their time. Overload is seen as the dragon, the external force that it seems impossible to overcome.

But the reality is that it's your demons – your own limiting beliefs, fears and hang-ups – that are the root cause of your overload and inability to make time for the most strategic activity. You cannot slay the dragon of overwhelm and busyness without first identifying and confronting your inner mindset demons.

In this part, you've seen this truth close up. You've observed how the stories we tell ourselves about what's necessary, possible and desirable create the world in which we think we live.

So, name your demon. Call it out from the shadows, where it can be mastered.

If it's your high standards, it's time to stop being the High-Performing Janitor and lean into the messiness of being the learner again. There's no learning in the comfort zone!

If it's your tendency to people-please, remember that it's actually undermining your ability to make your most unique and significant contribution. You think you're being a trustworthy and reliable team player, but actually you're simply taking the easy route, and not stepping up and leading with your greatest impact.

Even your sense of service becomes a demon when it's left unchecked. If you suffer from over-responsiveness, getting distracted by a thousand minor requests, remember you are important, your time is precious and it doesn't serve the greater good to have it scattered in so many directions.

If your demon is that need to control things, stop thinking 'can I delegate more?' and start thinking '*how* can I delegate more?' What will it look like to trust and develop your team?

If your demon is being driven and restless, and never taking time out of the action to think and be creative, then remember that your next level of success won't come from more productivity, but more creativity and thoughtfulness. You can't shift gear when your foot is jammed on the accelerator.

Name your demon. Say it out loud, and write it down. *The fear that is keeping me locked into busyness is…*

STAYING BUSY IS EASY

When I was about five years old, I read a book at school that I remember to this day. It was about a boy who was frightened of a black cat. He was told that the only way to overcome his fear was to go towards the cat. But one day he found himself alone, and the cat appeared. Frightened, the boy ran away, and the cat gave chase, getting bigger and bigger as it ran until it towered over him, an enormous and terrifying predator. The chase continued until the boy found himself cornered, with nowhere to run.

Then the boy remembered what his mother had told him. He turned to face the enormous cat. The cat froze. Taking his courage in his hands, he shakily took a step towards it. The enormous feline shrunk, ever so slightly. Another step. The cat shrunk again. And it continued; the boy walked towards the cat and by the time the boy was able to touch the animal it was just a tiny, cute black kitten. The boy picked up the cat and calmly walked home.

Our world of infinite demands gives us a convenient excuse to hide from our demons; we just blame the dragon of our busyness. Staying busy is easy; taking the steps to break through our wall of fear requires courage.

Staying busy is easy; taking the steps to break through our wall of fear requires courage.

Be like the boy in the story. Turn in the direction of your fear, and face it. The reality is that if we continually pursue our greatest contribution, we will be in a far stronger position than if we stay trapped within our fears.

In this part, we also looked at who you need to be for the next season. You created your to-be list, you've asked yourself WWXD, and you've set your volume and tone dials. So before moving forward make sure you've put your to-be list somewhere you're going to see it, as a reminder to be the person who overcomes their demons and gets to slay the dragon.

WHEELS WITHIN WHEELS

'I saw something that looked like a wheel on the ground beside each of the four-faced creatures. This is what the wheels looked like: They were identical wheels, sparkling like diamonds in the sun. It looked like they were wheels within wheels, like a gyroscope.'
– Book of Ezekiel (The Message version)

There are wheels within wheels. One secret of this book is that it applies at different levels. It applies to the self, but also to the team, to the sub-organisation, and to the entire company. Entire businesses have 'high-value activities' and 'top improvement projects'; they have mindset challenges and 'perfect systems for being crazy-busy' and 'commitment inventories', just as individuals do!

The culture around meetings, messaging, projects and priorities is nothing more than a system that's evolved over time. And so, as a leader, one of the highest value activities you can undertake is making system-level interventions.

You can take the exact concepts you've implemented at a personal level and use them to shape the culture of your team, your department or your business. You can create a leadership environment where focus and maximal contribution are promoted, and where distraction and noise are continually designed out of the system.

And that's precisely what we're going to look at in the final part of this book: the Environment Challenge.

Alternatively, you can choose your own adventure by heading back to page 28 and use the questions there – or the online assessment on the Xquadrant website – to decide what your next priority area needs to be.

> *To determine where your next focus area should be, we recommend using the online tool available at https://xquadrant.com/bookbonuses/*

Part 5

THE ENVIRONMENT CHALLENGE

CHAPTER 42

You say *agile*. I say *chaos*

In other parts of this book we have talked about the importance of making time to work on your most valuable activities and projects. You've built a plan to create Strategic Time, identified the conversations you need to have with your stakeholders to create new and more productive working agreements, and you've examined the mindset issues that have been keeping you stuck until now. These insights and strategies will allow you to free up substantial time to focus on more strategic activities.

However, this is just the beginning. If you want to truly see the power of Strategic Time in your organisation, you'll need to multiply it across your team, your department and beyond.

> *If you want to truly see the power of Strategic Time in your organisation, you'll need to multiply it across your team, your department and beyond.*

Let's face it: many companies have created a culture of distraction and busywork.

Ruth, a client of mine who's a marketing executive in a global technology distributor, spotted this in her organisation. 'I've made great progress in my own focus and on my high-value activities,' she said. 'But I've realised my organisation is addicted to firefighting! Every new idea, every new project needs to be done by yesterday. Every customer request becomes an "all hands on deck" moment. The expectation is that everyone is constantly checking email and messaging. We call it "being agile", but in reality it's just a lack of discipline.'

Exactly. As Tim Ferriss said in *Tools of Titans*: 'Being busy is most often used as a guise for avoiding the few critically important but uncomfortable actions.'

Cal Newport, author of *A World Without Email*, describes this as 'the hyperactive hive mind workflow'. He goes on to explain in an interview in *Fortune* that lots of organisations default to collaborating in the following way: '"Let's just work things out on the fly. We'll just rock and roll on email. We'll just rock and roll on Slack – unstructured, ad hoc, back and forth messaging, you can just figure things out." When you use that as the primary means by which you collaborate on most work that happens in your organisation, it simply doesn't scale.'

The question becomes:

'How can I encourage a culture of strategic focus, where we get the whole business out of the Infinity Trap, and promote Strategic Time?'

That's the Environment Challenge, and it's what we're going to tackle next.

CHAPTER 43

Work the system

Here's a story I was told about Howard Schultz, CEO of Starbucks. I haven't been able to verify its authenticity, but the insight is still there.

Schultz was visiting one of his Starbucks branches. This was a big deal for the store staff and everyone was looking forward to his arrival. As he got out of his car, Schultz's eyes were drawn to the illuminated Starbucks sign hanging over the polished glass front of the coffee shop. One of the bulbs had gone, so half the word wasn't lit up. Not the best first impression!

What did Schultz do in this moment? What would *you* have done?

He could have berated the store manager for his lack of attention to detail. He could have ranted in front of the whole staff, telling them that they should all have pride in the brand and take the initiative when they saw this kind of issue. He could have ordered someone to get up and change the bulb immediately. Or he could have found a ladder and done the job himself, to make the point.

He did none of these things. Instead he pulled out his phone and called up his Operations Director. 'Quick question for you,' he began. 'What's our process for blown bulbs on our signage?'

In this moment Schultz took a step away from the Ceiling of Complexity. He could have used time by fixing the one-off problem. Instead, he invested time and fixed the system so that this particular problem would never cause an issue again.

ASKING THE SYSTEMIC QUESTIONS

As we've seen, your own attention and focus is determined by the (generally invisible) systems you've put in place. Your system for email, your system for meetings, your system for saying yes (or no) to new projects and assignments, your system for managing your focus time, and so forth.

In a similar way, your entire organisation is running on systems within systems. The culture around meetings, messaging, projects and priorities is nothing more than a system that's evolved over time. And so, as a leader, one of the highest value activities you can undertake is making system-level interventions. Yet another reason why it's so important to free yourself up for Strategic Time!

So start keeping your eyes open for the systemic obstacles, those specific dynamics within the business that are getting in the way of leaders making time for strategy. Systemic obstacles could include incentives, decision-making structures, process requirements, the division of responsibilities, the strategic planning and prioritisation process, the requirements of particular IT systems, pressure by certain stakeholder groups, and so forth.

You might want to start asking around: 'What are the biggest systemic and structural drains on our time and attention that are stopping us from focusing on our top priorities?' You might find it's due to a whole bunch of projects of secondary importance. It might be due to duplicate work or manually entering data. It might be the current need to handle an unstructured stream of inbound requests from customers or colleagues. It might be the time and effort involved in scheduling and rescheduling appointments. It might be the fact that priorities shift so frequently that nobody gets time to actually complete any project before they're asked to drop everything to work on the next one.

At the same time, get people thinking about systemic solutions. You might be able to temporarily fix some of this by applying CRASH. But the bigger game is to fix the system, and address the key processes, incentives, responsibilities, ways of thinking, and resourcing decisions that are at play. You can kick this off with specific questions such as: 'What's broken in our project prioritisation system that leads us to have so many projects on the go at once?' 'What's our process to make sure that a whim from any one of us doesn't distract the teams from the projects that we've committed to for the quarter?' 'How can we stop every department constantly bombarding IT with feature requests?'

Make a list of the top five systemic obstacles preventing you and your people more from fully engaging in Strategic Time.

CHAPTER 44

Six barriers to IMPACT

The challenge, then, is collective and systemic transformation. We want people around us to start behaving in new ways (even when we're not looking!). We know that even changing our own behaviour is hard, so we shouldn't underestimate the challenge of doing it at scale.

What I've found through my own experience, as well as in my role of coaching CEOs and other top-level leaders, is that behaviour change occurs when a number of factors are in place. When one of these factors is weak or missing, behaviour change is incredibly difficult.

To help with this, I developed a mental model that I call The IMPACT Framework™. There are six barriers to impactful behaviour change. Any one of them can become a bottleneck and prevent change from occurring. Address them all, and change comes relatively easily. Here they are, along with the related question (from the point of view of the person or entity needing or wanting to change).

Insight. Do I know what I need to work on? If I'm not sure what specific shift to make, nothing is going to happen.

Motivation. Am I genuinely motivated to make this shift? Do I have an emotional engagement and an internal commitment to change?

Prompt. Is there an obvious trigger to prompt me to engage in this behaviour? And am I being prompted to practise this behaviour regularly enough to actually develop a new habit or skill? For example, if I want to develop my sales skills but I have no opportunities to sell anything, this is going to be a problem.

Ability. Am I able to behave in the desired way? Do I have the time, the resources, the skills in order to succeed at this? It's really important to make the target behaviour easy enough to do *even when motivation inevitably dips*.

Consequences. Do the consequences of this behaviour really matter? Is there an intrinsic payoff, a meaningful incentive, or an effective accountability structure to help me follow through?

Timeline. Is there a reason I need to be working on this *now*? If we're not convinced there's any time pressure for the behavioural shifts we're considering, we'll likely defer the hard work of change until it rises up our priority list.

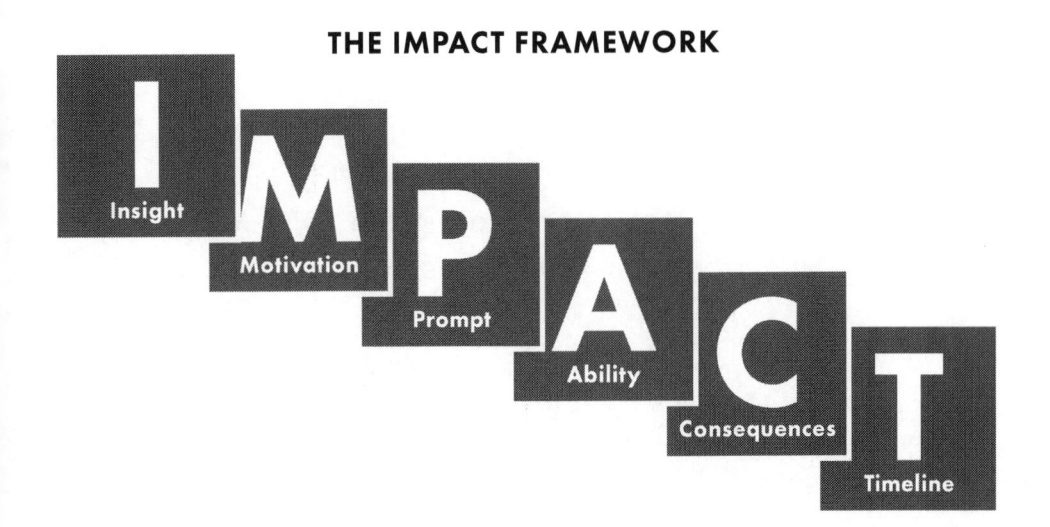

THE IMPACT FRAMEWORK

I - Insight
M - Motivation
P - Prompt
A - Ability
C - Consequences
T - Timeline

Whilst this model is fantastic to apply to your own personal development, in this part we're going to use The IMPACT Framework to help you lead your wider organisation from busywork to focus. You'll work through each barrier to IMPACT, one by one, and by dismantling the obstacles in turn you'll start to release the power of Strategic Time in your business.

START WITH A MICROCOSM

If you want to create a focus on Strategic Time in your organisational culture, you'll need to learn the counterintuitive secret to transformation at scale.

The problem is that most leaders are pursuing organisation-wide transformation without having been able to transform themselves or their own team.

Instead, start incredibly small. Create a *microcosm* of the transformation you want to see. Learn how to overcome the six barriers of The IMPACT Framework, and create an environment that truly promotes strategic focus. And then multiply *that*.

> *Most leaders are pursuing organisation-wide transformation without having been able to transform themselves or their own team.*

Putting it another way, you need something healthy before you multiply it.

This is why you need to become the strategic leader you want to see more of, because, as leadership author John Maxwell puts it, the senior leader is the 'lid' on the whole organisation.

And this is why you need to create a culture of strategic focus in your top team, because no organisation can be healthier than its #1 team. If your top team isn't making time to think or be strategic, and is overwhelmed in the details, then what chance does the rest of the organisation have?

Very often, leaders and leadership teams try to transform everyone else before doing the real work on themselves. And they wonder why they meet resistance and cynicism!

So, be very specific about the microcosm that you want to begin the transformation with. It's probably your team of direct reports, but make a definite choice now. And now you've got that group very clearly in mind, ask yourself:

Which of the six barriers to IMPACT is the most immediate limiting factor for the microcosm you want to focus on right now?

CHAPTER 45

Words are your weapon

'I feel so inar, inar, inar, inar, inar, inar, inar, inar – ticulate!' – Freddie Mercury

At the heart of the Environment Challenge is a cultural shift. You are shaping your team or company culture into one where focus and maximal contribution are promoted, and where distraction and noise are continually engineered out of the ways of working.

Culture is what people do when no one's looking. It's the shared assumptions, mindset and, most critically, the behaviours that people have learned will make them successful, in a certain context (such as a family, or a firm, or a team).

Often we can't see the culture we're in; it just feels 'normal' to us. As the fish said, 'Water? What water?' We often only understand our culture by way of comparison. When we travel to the other side of the world we realise how specific our home culture actually is, and when we change company we discover that their values and habits are very different from our previous firm.

Without insight, nothing will change. Unless the people in your organisation share an understanding of what Strategic Time is, and why it matters, you're never going to be able to embed it.

So it's time to bring out the power tool. Language. To change the culture, change the words.

In reading this book, you've expanded your vocabulary. You understand the *Infinity Trap* and the *Ceiling of Complexity*. The distinction between *Using Time* and *Investing Time*. You've internalised the importance of *Strategic Time* and have focused yourself on your *High-Value Activities* and an *Improvement Project*. You've done your *Commitment Inventory* and applied *CRASH*. You understand the *TIME* model for freeing yourself up, and you're working through *The IMPACT Framework*.

All these words carry weight and power. Power to shift your thinking and power to alter your behaviour. And to build a culture of true focus, where Strategic Time is understood and valued, you need to embed these same words in your organisation.

Our words shape our world and sculpt our culture.

Our words shape our world and sculpt our culture. They allow us to communicate complex thoughts with just a syllable or two. They give us reference points and distinctions we didn't have before. Every discipline, every culture and every organisation harnesses language to create a common outlook and focus collective attention.

And so your job is actually simple, though not always easy. Teach your organisation the language of strategic focus. Use the words yourself, and explain them. Train your people to grow awareness of this new vocabulary at scale. And help them move from a passive vocabulary (which they understand but don't use) to an active vocabulary (which they actively use in their working life to make decisions, question their assumptions, and refocus their attention).

Teaching your organisation a new vocabulary might feel odd at first, but it's simpler than you might think. In many ways it's as simple as starting to use the key terms and concepts regularly in your own conversation. Here are some ideas to speed up the process:

- » Run a lunch-and-learn session for your team.
- » Set up a workshop to explore these ideas.
- » Buy your colleagues a copy of this book, and then set up a call to discuss it.
- » Invite Xquadrant to run a seminar or workshop for your organisation.

Or you can just start to share these ideas, colleague by colleague. One discussion at a time, start to surface the ways the organisational culture promotes over-responsiveness and busywork and gets in the way of strategic focus.

Start a conversation about the value of strategic time, and introduce the language and ideas into your environment.

> *Remember, there are plenty of helpful tools to help your wider organisation make TIME for strategy on our website: https://xquadrant.com/bookbonuses/*

CHAPTER 46

What are we not getting to?

If your team or organisation has started to understand the value of Strategic Time, you've dealt with the insight barrier and you're now faced with the question of motivation.

Insight without motivation is an intellectual assent without emotional engagement. It's awareness without commitment. It's knowing you should lose a few pounds but not wanting to diet. It's knowing you should get into shape but not joining a gym. And it's understanding that it would be good to spend more time working on the next-level projects, without wanting to do the real work involved in extracting yourself from all the noise.

How can you raise the motivation levels of your team or organisation to deal with the cultural and systemic issues that are keeping people trapped in pointless meetings and other distractions, and away from the high-value work that will make a difference?

Once again, the answer will be found in conversation. You'll need to help the group:

- » Clarify the stakes
- » Paint the picture
- » Explore the resistance

CLARIFY THE STAKES

Clarifying the stakes involves tapping into pleasure and pain, desire and fear, in order to really understand and draw out the difference between 'the best case if we act on this' and 'the worst case if we don't'.

There's an art to this conversation. You're alternating between the light and the dark, the factors that inspire us and the fears that push us to act. To move from insight to motivation, it's important to get beyond the intellectual assent and evoke a visceral, emotional response.

Here are the kinds of questions you might want to ask to help your team clarify the stakes:

- » *'What is our culture of "always be checking your messages" costing you personally? What's it costing us as a business?'*
- » *'What's one really important project that we're not getting to right now as a team, and what's that costing us?'*
- » *'If we could free ourselves and our teams up from some of those pointless meetings we all attend, what would that enable us to create?'*
- » *'If we could wave a magic wand and cut the least valuable 50 per cent of projects, what difference would that make to you and to your team?'*

PAINT THE PICTURE

It's hard to get motivated by a fuzzy or unclear destination. So in your conversation you need to draw out of people a clear vision of what a more focused, strategic organisation really looks like – and what it allows them to accomplish.

The tools from Part 1 will be useful here. Have the conversation about your collective HVAs (high-value activities) and desired outcomes.

'If we could extract ourselves/help our managers extract themselves from operational minutiae, what would that allow us to accomplish?'

'What is the one Improvement Project that, if we could deliver it in the next ninety days, would make everything else we're doing as a team so much easier?'

Remember, you can't free yourself up *from* things, but you can free yourself up *for* things. Until your leaders are clear on what the critical deliverables are, everything feels equally important.

EXPLORE THE RESISTANCE

The reality is that individuals, teams and organisations find themselves stuck in a certain pattern of behaviour because there's some kind of payoff, benefit or convenience to it. So when it comes to releasing motivation, it's important to drill into what the motivations are for keeping the status quo, and to help the team put these out into the open, where their emotional hold will start to lessen.

Exploring the resistance involves two things: facing the discrepancy and counting the cost. Facing the discrepancy involves observing that we're saying one thing and doing another, and probing: what's really going on there? Counting the cost involves surfacing what we're going to have to give up to attain what we say we want, and deciding if we're truly ready to let those things go.

Here are some example questions to help you detect and engage with the resistance in your chosen microcosm.

'We know that pinging people on Slack all the time distracts them and stops them focusing, but we still all do it. What gives?'

'We say we've had enough of firefighting, but we've still not got around to building the processes to prevent the issues. What's the actual benefit of firefighting to us, what's the payoff, that keeps us coming back to that way of working?'

'We say we all want more strategic time and focus, but what will we need to give up in order to achieve that? Are we really ready to make that sacrifice?'

MOTIVATION IS FICKLE

Motivation is always in flux. Some days we're motivated, others we're less so. That's fine. As you dismantle the barrier of motivation in your business, what you're looking for is an emotional pull and commitment amongst your leadership to the idea of helping the business truly make time for strategic activity.

Start to draw out the emotional commitment of your team to the journey ahead, by clarifying the stakes, painting the picture and exploring the resistance.

CHAPTER 47

Remove the chocolate from the mini-bar

'I can resist anything except temptation.' – Oscar Wilde

A colleague of mine once checked into a hotel, only to find an extensive selection of chocolates and other treats laid out in the room. As he had an ongoing commitment to eating healthily, his normal policy was to immediately call reception and ask them to remove the goodies. On this occasion he decided to trust in his own willpower. He simply slid the tray under the bed, out of sight. 'I'm a strong and successful leader,' he thought, 'and I can easily resist some chocolates for the three days of this conference.'

You can guess the end of the story. On day one, he successfully resisted. On day two, all good. On day three the tray came out and the chocolates were promptly devoured!

At this point, your team understands the value of building an organisation where leaders make time for strategy (insight), and they're excited to move forward and create the conditions for doing so (motivation).

But, insight and motivation aren't enough. Any attempts to shift organisational behaviour through collective willpower is doomed. As we've said before, motivation is fickle. You can't rely on that. Instead, you need to create an environment that will make the rise of Strategic Time almost inevitable.

As the story above shows, our environment determines our behaviour to a far larger degree than we'd like to admit. This is why so many good ideas coming out of annual team offsite meetings end up going nowhere: the insight and motivation is there, but the environment hasn't changed, and so everyone falls back into the same old habits very quickly once the buzz of the team meeting has faded.

I want to challenge you to move towards a 'zero-effort' environment, where the right behaviour comes naturally. 'Zero-effort' might seem a stretch, but that's the goal. And we build this environment by turning our attention to the next three conditions for success in The IMPACT Framework: Prompt, Ability and Consequences, which will each reinforce the power of the environment in which the team operates.

SEED THE ENVIRONMENT WITH PROMPTS

Your zero-effort environment needs to provide clear prompts for the behaviours you want to establish. The key question for your team is likely to be:

'When, specifically, do we expect people to do their deep, undistracted work? And how can we prompt that?'

Often we skim over the need to seed the environment with prompts. We assume that flexibility is the best solution, and we let people figure out the best moment for them to carve out Strategic Time and other desired behaviours. But total flexibility makes it much harder to create an environment that actively prompts and triggers that behaviour, and it makes it harder to establish an organisational culture. If one person is trying to carve out space to think precisely at the moment that their boss is in full 'get through my to-do list mode', there's likely to be a clash.

A strong environmental prompt would actually be a specific and shared time slot for strategic time: 'Tuesdays from 9–11 is our team's strategic time – email is to be closed, notifications switched off, and no conflicting calls are to be scheduled in this period.'

You might find some other prompts to establish, based on whatever obstacles to Strategic Time you've discovered in your organisation. For example, if the leadership team needs to review and prune the list of corporate initiatives once per month, then what's the specific prompt for that?

> *Creating shared rhythms is an important step in building a zero-effort environment. Make sure your culture supports strategic time, instead of undermining it.*

You might be thinking that mandating specific time slots for specific activities feels suboptimal, and managers should do whatever works best for them. Remember, however, that we're trying here to create an environment that supports Strategic Time and eliminates busywork, pointless meetings and constant distraction – and the status quo has clearly not been working for many managers. Moreover, companies are continually shaping the working rhythm of their employees – from specifying working hours to fixing reporting schedules and numerous other deadlines. And many firms have recently introduced initiatives such as 'no meeting days' with a good deal of success. Creating shared rhythms is an important step in building a zero-effort environment. Make sure your culture supports strategic time, instead of undermining it.

As you engage the team in this discussion about *when* strategic time should be happening, think about what prompts can be built in to promote that behaviour. I call this 'seeding the environment'. Here are a couple of options:

Meeting agendas. Meeting agendas are great prompts for action. If we have a review or a report to give, we're likely to create time for whatever needs to happen.

Communications. Emails and messages can serve as helpful prompts if used wisely. Perhaps set these up in advance, so you know they'll reliably be sent out.

Physical cues. Old-school techniques like posters, notices and boards can work in some cases, although their effect tends to diminish over time as people get used to them and start to ignore them.

Mutual signalling. Identify ways you can signal to each other that you're in focus mode and doing the deep work, so that your colleagues know not to interrupt you. Some software developers do this by wearing headphones whilst they're deep in code to signal to others in the office that they're concentrating hard. Other people I know put a sign on the door, or make some other simple physical change to their office environment to flag the same idea. You may need to set your online presence status as well, or log out of chat, so colleagues won't disturb you there.

Collectively decide when you'll engage in Strategic Time, and how you can seed the environment with unmissable prompts.

CHAPTER 48

Clear, quick, convenient

A zero-effort environment has to make it easy for people to perform the desired behaviours, and hard for them to engage in undesired behaviours. To use an analogy, if there are healthy snacks in the kitchen and the cupboards have been stripped of junk food then healthy eating becomes almost inevitable.

So, let's move on to the Ability part of The IMPACT Framework, and engage your team in a discussion about ability and ease:

'What is making it hard for our people to say "no" to low-value activities, and what is making it hard for them to say "yes" to making time for high-value projects?'

Take it one step at a time. You're looking for perhaps one critical behaviour to promote, and one undesirable behaviour to discourage. And then, find as many ways to make it fun and easy to engage in the first behaviour as possible, and find ways to make it inconvenient to engage in the second.

Generally speaking, things are easy when they're clear, quick, convenient and when there aren't any temptations. They're difficult when they're ambiguous, take a long time, require resources that aren't immediately at hand, and are subject to getting derailed by temptations present in the environment.

Make it clearer. Define the goal. Have upfront discussions to scope out exactly what needs to be done.

This is essential. What's the actual behaviour that you're tackling? Is it learning to use SCARS to improve problem-solving with your teams? Is it applying TRADE to avoid being dragged into pointless meetings? Is it applying the CRASH methodology? Carving out Forts for Strategic Time, or Prisons for admin time? Get specific on the one habit you're trying to institutionalise, and help people understand what exactly they will do.

Are we clear on exactly what we will do?

How we will know when we can 'declare success' and move to another task?

Make it quicker. Shrink scope until it becomes embarrassingly easy to do! For example, rather than committing to sixty minutes of strategic time each day, make the goal ten minutes and take it from there.

What's a tiny version of our desired behaviour?

What's the minimum viable task here?

How can we streamline this?

Behavioural expert BJ Fogg, professor at Stanford and author of *Tiny Habits,* used this approach to build a habit of press-ups, by committing to do just two press-ups at various points in the day. He would declare success after these two repetitions, but once he was down on the ground in position, he often found himself doing ten or twenty or more. However, if he'd set the larger number as the goal, he wouldn't have had the motivation to actually begin.

Make it more convenient. Ensure the necessary resources are easily accessible at the point of need. Remove any friction associated with actually getting on with the task in question.

Are there any checklists, tools or templates we can provide?

Are there any meetings that we need to set up to facilitate this task?

Who else in the organisation needs to support this endeavour?

Runners use this technique when they lay out their running gear the night before, so when they wake up it's incredibly convenient to immediately get dressed and hit the road.

Remove temptations. Take the chocolate out of the kitchen! Think about the most likely distractions and temptations and consider how you'll remove those. One common temptation involves the notifications on your computer or phone, since it's incredibly hard to stay focused on deep work when you see a new message come in. Create a culture where notifications are turned off, and responsiveness is managed in other ways. Another common temptation is the new project or new priority that distracts the team from the agreed strategy. You might want to consider how those incoming requests can be thoughtfully reviewed and assessed before people commit to them.

What are the distractions that will take us off track?

Is there a specific time we need to ring-fence, to avoid conflicts?

How do we end up inadvertently distracting each other?

When you combine these tactics, you greatly improve the chances of instilling a new behaviour, because the environment is now working for you and not against you. Here's an example.

Let's say you want everyone in your team to ring-fence three hours of Strategic Time each week. It's not particularly clear – frankly they're not quite sure what to do with this 'strategic thinking time', making it highly likely they'll default to more urgent tasks instead (like using the time as a buffer to catch up on email). Time feels quite challenging – can they move straight away from nothing to three hours? And there are plenty of temptations, as they keep getting distracted by calls, meetings and messages.

To make it clear, perhaps ask people on your Monday team call exactly what they want to use their Strategic Time block for in the coming week, so they have already given some thought to their intention for that time and why it matters. Add an agenda point to the weekly meeting template to ensure this question is never forgotten.

To make it quick, perhaps agree as a team to find just thirty minutes per week instead of three hours.

And to remove temptations, inform the rest of the organisation that your department is not available during the specified period. Have a team 'tech session' where everyone sets up their electronic devices to turn notifications off for the desired time period each week.

How can you create an environment that makes your desired behaviours easy, quick and convenient? And what temptations and distractions will you collectively remove from your environment?

CHAPTER 49

Making it matter

Consequences, the fifth element of The IMPACT Framework, matter because we naturally gravitate to activities that give us some kind of payoff. Part of the art of leadership is creating an environment that creates tangible and emotional consequences that support the behaviours needed for the organisation to thrive.

In discussion with your team, look at your environment to reinforce consequences at three levels – internal, interpersonal and external.

Internal consequences: How can we make the new behaviours inherently satisfying and rewarding?

Habit expert James Clear points out in his fascinating book *Atomic Habits* that every successful habit has to be *satisfying*. There has to be some kind of immediate payoff for the individual – for example, the 'feel good' moment of completing something on our to-do list or finally getting that project out the door.

So, let's imagine your team realises it needs to make some hard choices about resource allocation between projects, and decides to initiate a monthly meeting to do that. To make that meeting more satisfying, you might decide to end each meeting with a round of applause for yourselves, for having the courage to make those tough decisions. It might feel forced, but you're actually creating an important feel-good factor that encourages people to come back for more.

Interpersonal consequences. How can we recognise and celebrate each other's progress?

Celebration and recognition is an extremely powerful driver of behaviour. So what are the opportunities to celebrate the efforts that each person makes to streamline their diary and lean into more strategic work?

Team calls or all-hands meetings are great forums for this. Ask who's made time for strategic work this week, and celebrate what they managed to achieve. Ask for people to share what's working for them as they shift their focus to higher-value work.

Celebration is even more powerful when it's unexpected. I know a leader who sends his team flowers when they fail, to thank them for pushing the boundaries and being bold in their action. It sends a powerful message. In a similar vein, instead of getting irritated when a colleague pushes back on attending your project meeting, why not congratulate them for prioritising their strategic work and making the hard decision?

External consequences. Is there sufficient accountability and incentive in place to support this behaviour change?

External consequences can involve the typical tools of rewards and punishments, but the bigger question is about closing the loop on what people commit to. Is anyone actually watching, and does anyone actually care? Is there really any sense of accountability – or is this just a nice-to-have idea that can be safely discarded without real-world consequences?

You might not have the necessary authority to impose the 'carrot and the stick' on your colleagues, but other avenues are open. Invite them to make a clear and documented promise, and agree a specific moment where their follow-through on that promise will be reviewed.

SET THE TIMELINE FOR COMPLETION

This brings us naturally to the final element of the IMPACT model, Timeline. Consequences only make sense where there's a clear sense of timing. And as every manager knows, a project without a finish date is just a vague intention.

So establish a clear commitment to a timeline. You know what the picture of success looks like – what's the due date for it to be in place by? If you can't agree on the timeline, you probably don't have a clear and meaningful goal yet.

When are your environmental changes going to be done?

When are your team behaviours going to be the norm?

Put a date on it. And monitor it like you would any other project.

How will you create an environment with real consequences? What are the celebrations, incentives and accountability structures to support the move to Strategic Time? And when will it be done?

CHAPTER 50

Roadmap to revolution

In this part, you've realised that the TIME methodology doesn't just apply at an individual level. You've discovered the game-changing impact that results when an entire organisation – a team, a department and ultimately an entire corporation – gets serious about making time for strategic activity.

You've seen how even minor system-level interventions can have an outsized effect on business performance, and you've resisted the urge to 'go big or go home' and instead focused in on a microcosm. Change how that entity operates, and then make the case for a larger transformation.

In other words: change the environment, change everything.

You've also learned a systematic way to remove the barriers associated with behaviour change, The IMPACT Framework.

Because Insight is the starting point, you'll be engaging people in conversations and introducing the notion of Strategic Time, and how it can catapult organisations over the current Ceiling of Complexity that they're facing.

Rather than jumping straight in to action, you've learned to test Motivation, by creating a shared clarity around what benefits the organisation can generate and what the necessary sacrifice is going to have to be.

You'll then identify and establish some organisational Prompts, to trigger the new behaviour that you want instead of it getting forgotten amongst the thousand other things going on right now.

Collectively, you'll ensure everyone has an Ability to engage in Strategic Time. You've thought through simple ways to make it easy. And you'll reinforce this behaviour through Consequences – celebrating success and maintaining accountability.

Finally, you'll establish a Timeline to get to your desired endpoint. You'll commit to streamlining your Commitment Inventory together, perhaps by applying the CRASH methodology.

There it is. The beginnings of a pragmatic roadmap that can lead to a revolution in how your team, business unit and organisation allocates their time, and in the impact they create.

There's a lot of work involved in bringing about real change at scale in a business. If you'd like some help in implementing these ideas personally, in your team, or in your wider organisation, please do get in touch.

If you've been reading the book linearly, you're pretty much done, and you can turn the page and enjoy the concluding chapter. Alternatively, you might want to continue your adventure into Strategic Time by heading back to page 28 and use the questions there (or our online assessment on the Xquadrant website) to decide what your next priority area needs to be.

CONCLUSION

CHAPTER 51

Two Paths

***You can't change gear when your foot
is jammed on the accelerator.***

In this book I've argued that you, your team and your organisation all have an infinite amount of demands on your time, creating a permanent state of overload. All around, you see people attempting to cram even more into their day, trying and failing to make a dent in their never-ending workload by simply becoming more productive.

But your eyes have been opened. You have seen the Infinity Trap for what it is. It's a seductive temptation to get caught in busyness, succumb to tunnel vision, and make incremental progress on a million operational tasks without creating the fresh insights or making the transformational moves that will change everything.

A fork has opened up in the road. Two paths, and two destinies. Which will you choose?

Most leaders take the familiar path of *using time*, of working harder and harder… and coming up against the Ceiling of Complexity. It's actually a comfortable path even though it's tiring, because it's familiar and it relies on the skills that made us successful in the past. I invite you to commit to the other path, the way of *investing time*. It's the path where you work on your #1 Improvement Project to create Strategic Time and double down on your high-value activities.

Most leaders take the familiar path of trying to make tiny improvements in their use of time. I invite you to commit to the other path, the way of making bold decisions to free up time in the short term, and of implementing ongoing structures, systems and habits to help you continue to avoid the low-value tasks over time.

Most leaders take the familiar path of trying to level up in isolation, and they end up struggling to make meaningful change. I invite you to commit to the other path. Influence the people around you, create powerful agreements so that your new focus is supported and welcomed by your broader organisation, and 'raise energy barriers' to shift the organisational dynamics. This is the path of leadership, where you create new possibilities for greater impact one conversation at a time.

Most leaders take the familiar path of blaming external factors for their busyness. They believe they have no choice given all the pressures and demands on their time. I invite you to commit to the other path, where you accept that those factors aren't really to blame after all. This other path means discovering that the root cause of your overload and inability to make time for the most strategic topics lies within. It's the path where you address the fears, the people-pleasing, and the unconscious assumptions that are keeping you on the hamster wheel.

Finally, most leaders take the familiar path of trying to improve their own productivity and protect their team from the biggest distractions of the wider organisation. I invite you to commit to the other path, the path of shaping the environment around you, shifting the culture and working on the system-level fixes that will improve strategic focus firstly within your team and then within your wider business.

We've covered many ideas, tools and strategies in this book, but there's one core theme. That theme is courage, which is at the heart of what it means to be a leader. Courage to start working on higher-value activities. Courage to own your busyness, and face the fears that are driving you to say 'yes' to the infinite demands around you. Courage to step out of the low-value work. And courage to have the bold conversations with those around you.

You are a competent and capable leader. Take the second path; pursue your greatest contribution with courage and commitment, and let the demands of infinity flow smoothly past you.

The outcome will be remarkable.

Next Steps

If you've enjoyed *Making Time For Strategy*, here are some ways to continue your journey.

Explore the book bonuses. They are complimentary and will help you turn the ideas in the book into action. https://xquadrant.com/bookbonuses

Follow along. Sign up for the Xquadrant Insider for a weekly email to help you shift from incremental thinking to exponential impact; follow me on LinkedIn; or check out my podcast, The Impact Multiplier CEO.

Share your insights. Please consider leaving a brief review on Amazon. It would really help me spread the word, it will help future readers make an informed decision, and it will help you to distil your insights and consolidate your own learning.

Bring the message to your leaders. If you're looking for a practical, challenging and inspiring workshop for your leadership team meeting or a keynote speech at your corporate retreat, then get in touch.

Join one of our programmes. Let's face it, reading a book gives us inspiration and information - but real transformation is far easier when you have personalised support. If you're committed to leading more impactfully and strategically, our programmes provide the coaching, community and accountability to create a sustained shift in how you operate as a leader.

Work with me personally. If you're a successful entrepreneur or high-level executive who is committed to multiplying your impact even further, then let's talk. I work with some of the world's top leaders to help them attain new heights, including CEOs of multi-billion corporations, founders of tech 'unicorns', and other extraordinary high achievers.

Of course, our business moves infinitely faster than the pages in a book, so why not head over to https://xquadrant.com/ to discover more, or strike up a conversation at richard@xquadrant.com ?

ABOUT THE AUTHOR

Richard Medcalf is a trusted coach and advisor to some of the most successful founders and CEOs on the planet. He helps them and their teams reinvent their success formula, so that they multiply their impact and achieve breakthrough results. Top of his year at Oxford University, and subsequently a Partner in a global strategy consultancy and a senior executive at tech giant Cisco, he is the founder of leadership consultancy Xquadrant. Richard has advised the C-Suite for over 25 years, with clients ranging from Fortune 50 corporations to the world's most exciting hyper growth tech firms. British-born, he's lived in France for over two decades. He is happily married and the proud father of two. Richard describes himself as 'what you get if you were to put a McKinsey consultant, a slightly unorthodox pastor and an entrepreneur into a blender,' and has an insatiable love for spicy food.

Printed by Amazon Italia Logistica S.r.l.
Torrazza Piemonte (TO), Italy